one pound of imagination: main dishes

microwave cooking library®

by barbara methven

microwave cooking library®

"Now what do I do with it?" Have you ever wondered that as you picked up yet another package of chicken pieces or fish fillets at the supermarket? Chicken or fish may be your family's favorite food, but at times, you feel you've run out of ideas for cooking it.

If this sounds familiar, *One Pound of Imagination* is designed for you. Explore these creative ways to use the everyday foods you buy weekly. Start with one chicken, one pound of fish fillets, four pork chops or a can of beans, and turn each into a tasty, satisfying meal for four to six people. This book features page after page of ideas, from simple to elegant, that can work magic with ingredients you keep on hand — perfect when you have little time to cook and less time to shop.

Barbara Methven

Barbara Methven

CREDITS:
Design & Production: Cy DeCosse Incorporated
Senior Art Director: Delores Swanson
Art Director: Yelena Konrardy
Project Director: Peggy Ramette
Project Manager: Deborah Bialik
Home Economists: Sue Brue, Bonnie Ellingboe, Peggy Ramette, Ann Stuart, Grace Wells
Dietitian: Patricia D. Godfrey, R.D.
Consultants: Susanne C. Mattison, Barbara Strand, Grace Wells
Editors: Janice Cauley, Bernice Maehren
Director of Development Planning & Production: Jim Bindas
Production Manager: Amelia Merz
Electronic Publishing Analyst: Kevin D. Frakes
Production Staff: Joe Fahey, Melissa Grabanski, Jim Huntley, Mark Jacobson, Duane John, Daniel Meyers, Linda Schloegel, Greg Wallace, Nik Wogstad
Studio Manager: Rebecca DaWald
Photographers: Rex Irmen, John Lauenstein, Mark Macemon, Charles Nields, Mette Nielsen, Mike Parker, Cathleen Shannon
Food Stylists: Sue Brue, Bobbette Destiche
Color Separations: Scantrans
Printing: R. R. Donnelley & Sons (0391)

Additional volumes in the Microwave Cooking Library series are available from the publisher:

- Basic Microwaving
- Recipe Conversion for Microwave
- Microwaving Meats
- Microwave Baking & Desserts
- Microwaving Meals in 30 Minutes
- Microwaving on a Diet
- Microwaving Fruits & Vegetables
- Microwaving Convenience Foods
- Microwaving for Holidays & Parties
- Microwaving for One & Two
- The Microwave & Freezer
- 101 Microwaving Secrets
- Microwaving Light & Healthy
- Microwaving Poultry & Seafood
- Microwaving America's Favorites
- Microwaving Fast & Easy Main Dishes
- More Microwaving Secrets
- Microwaving Light Meals & Snacks
- Holiday Microwave Ideas
- Easy Microwave Menus
- Low-fat Microwave Meals
- Cool Quick Summer Microwaving
- Ground Beef Microwave Meals
- Microwave Speed Meals

CY DE COSSE INCORPORATED
Chairman: Cy DeCosse
President: James B. Maus
Executive Vice President: William B. Jones

Library of Congress Cataloging-in-Publication Data

Methven, Barbara
  One pound of imagination: main dishes / Barbara Methven.

    p.   cm. — (Microwave cooking library)
Includes index.
ISBN 0-86573-571-9

    1. Microwave cookery 2. Entrées (Cookery) I. Title. II. Series.
TX832.M4158   1991   90-28782
641.5'882 — dc20

the microwave cooking library,® 5900 green oak drive, p.o. box 3020, minnetonka, mn 55343

Dear Subscriber:

We're excited to send you <u>One Pound of Imagination: Main Dishes</u> ... just off the press as The Microwave Cooking Library's latest volume!

Here are dozens of creative ideas -- from the simple-and-fast to the elegant -- to help you make delicious and interesting dishes from "everyday" foods you buy weekly. Take a pound of chicken, fish, ground beef ... or some pork chops, a can of tuna or beans ... and turn it into something special <u>tonight</u>! You could make delightful Deep Dish Spaghetti Pie (p.15), fabulous Philly Chicken Sandwiches (p. 81), delicious and different BLT Fish Salad (p. 111) or special Sweet Potato Pancakes (p. 133)!

Get even more out of your entire Microwave Cooking Library with a Master Index to lead you to the recipes you want. Call Customer Service (number listed below) to order yours for only $2.95!

And once you've added some imagination to your weekly menu, you'll be ready for our new volume, <u>One Dish Meals</u>. You'll get this book late this fall -- a collection of nutritious, satisfying meals you can serve in a single dish. Every idea is delicious, and clean-up will be <u>so</u> easy!

But for now, enjoy <u>One Pound of Imagination: Main Dishes</u>. Thanks for your business! We're glad to have you as a customer.

Sincerely,

James Maus, Publisher

P.S. Any questions about your account? Want to order a **Master Index**? Call TOLL-FREE 1-800-328-3895 (9 a.m. to 4 p.m. CST, M-F) for friendly, reliable service.

5K

Contents

What You Need to Know Before You Start

Day after day, week after week, most meals start from a limited list of main ingredients. How do you make this week's chicken different from last week's chicken? What if you want to serve chicken twice in the same week? With imagination, you can vary your main dishes and make sure the family won't say "What? Chicken AGAIN?"

Start by expanding your list of basic protein sources. A glance at the table of contents in this book may suggest a few you rarely, if ever, consider when deciding what to fix for dinner. They are all everyday items, the kind you buy weekly or keep in your freezer or pantry.

Next consider how the meat, fish or other protein is cooked, what flavors it, what goes with it. Cooking procedure can change the taste, appearance and texture of a food. For example, microwaved fish fillets have a delicate flavor and moist texture. The same fillets can be coated with crumbs and oven baked for a dry, crunchy crust.

You can also cook the same food in the same way over and over again, but vary the results with imaginative seasonings and flavor combinations. No matter what kind of meatballs you make, the cooking procedure remains the same. The seasonings you put into the meatballs and the sauce that surrounds them create the difference.

Each section in this book deals with a familiar main ingredient in common units of measurement. Most day-to-day meal preparation starts when you go to your refrigerator, freezer or pantry and take out one chicken, a package of pork chops, a can of tuna or a cup of rice.

Four Kinds of Recipes

In addition to the familiar recipe format, this book offers three types of special recipes. The first is a basic recipe, followed by several supplementary recipes that use this basic dish. For example, Savory Pan-fried Chicken Strips create a main dish salad, a risotto or a stroganoff.

Once you decide how you will use the basic recipe, read the supplementary recipe carefully. There may be subtle changes in seasoning to complement this particular dish.

With the second type of recipe, you can achieve an entirely different effect by changing an ingredient or two. These variations on a theme follow the main recipe.

The third type is recipes printed in pairs. There is a family resemblance between the two, but methods, ingredients or results differ too much to consider them variations. For example, start with half a pound of deli pastrami or corned beef and produce either a traditional skillet hash or a super-fast microwave hash.

Nutritional Information

Per serving nutritional values follow each recipe. When a dish serves 4 to 6 persons, the analysis applies to the greater number of servings. In the case of alternate ingredients, such as margarine or butter, the analysis refers to the first ingredient listed. Where variations accompany the recipe, the analysis covers the original recipe, not the variations. Optional ingredients are not included in the nutritional analysis.

Meats

Steak &
Potato Stir-fry

Start with One Pound of Ground Beef

Versatile ground beef adapts to a variety of dishes—meatballs in distinctive sauces, stuffed vegetables, filled breads and hearty, full-meal casseroles.

Taco Meatballs

1 lb. lean ground beef, crumbled
1/3 cup unseasoned dry bread crumbs
1 egg
1 pkg. (1.25 oz.) taco seasoning mix

How to Make Taco Meatballs

Combine all ingredients in medium mixing bowl.

Shape into 20 meatballs, about 1 1/4 inches in diameter.

Saucy Mexican Meatballs

1 recipe Taco Meatballs (above)
1 can (14 1/2 oz.) diced tomatoes, drained (reserve juice)
1/4 cup canned chopped green chilies, drained
1/4 cup tomato paste
1/4 teaspoon sugar
Hot cooked rice
Shredded Cheddar cheese (optional)
Sliced green onions (optional)

4 servings

Prepare meatballs. Arrange in even layer in 8-inch square baking dish. Top with tomatoes and chilies. Microwave at High for 7 to 11 minutes, or until meatballs are firm and no longer pink, rearranging once. Using slotted spoon, remove meatballs. Cover meatballs to keep warm. Set aside.

Add reserved juice, the tomato paste and sugar to tomato mixture. Mix well. Microwave at High for 3 to 4 minutes, or until mixture thickens and bubbles, stirring twice. Add meatballs, turning to coat with sauce. Microwave at High for 2 to 3 minutes, or until hot, stirring meatballs once. Serve over rice. Sprinkle with cheese and onions.

◄ *Serving suggestion: Spoon meatballs and sauce into taco shells or over shredded-lettuce-lined tostada shells. Sprinkle with cheese and onions.*

Per Serving: Calories: 440 • Protein: 27 g. • Carbohydrate: 44 g. • Fat: 17 g.
• Cholesterol: 124 mg. • Sodium: 670 mg.
Exchanges: 2 starch, 2 medium-fat meat, 3 vegetable, 1 fat

Mexican Meatball Soup

1 recipe Taco Meatballs (above)
2 cups ready-to-serve chicken broth
1 cup water
1 jar (16 oz.) salsa
1 can (11 oz.) corn, drained
1 tablespoon snipped fresh cilantro

4 to 6 servings

Prepare meatballs. Arrange in single layer in 3-quart casserole. Microwave at High for 5 to 9 minutes, or until meatballs are firm and no longer pink, rearranging once. Drain. Add remaining ingredients. Cover. Microwave at High for 8 to 10 minutes, or until soup is hot, stirring once. Top each serving with coarsely crushed taco chips, if desired.

Per Serving: Calories: 250 • Protein: 18 g.
• Carbohydrate: 17 g. • Fat: 12 g.
• Cholesterol: 82 mg. • Sodium: 1050 mg.
Exchanges: 1/2 starch, 2 medium-fat meat, 2 vegetable, 1/2 fat

Meatball Stroganoff

Meatballs:

 1 lb. lean ground beef, crumbled
 1 egg
 ¼ cup unseasoned dry bread crumbs
 1 teaspoon Worcestershire sauce
 ¼ teaspoon garlic powder
 ¼ teaspoon freshly ground pepper

 1 can (4 oz.) mushroom stems and pieces, drained
 2 tablespoons white wine or ready-to-serve beef broth
 1 tablespoon all-purpose flour
 ½ cup ready-to-serve beef broth
 2 tablespoons tomato paste
 2 tablespoons sour cream
   Snipped fresh parsley (optional)
   Buttered egg noodles or hot cooked rice

4 servings

In medium mixing bowl, combine all meatball ingredients. Shape into 16 meatballs, about 1½ inches in diameter. Arrange in even layer in 8-inch square baking dish. Sprinkle with mushrooms and wine. Microwave at High for 8 to 10 minutes, or until meatballs are firm and no longer pink, rearranging once. Using slotted spoon, remove meatballs. Cover meatballs to keep warm. Set aside.

Stir flour into mixture in baking dish. Blend in broth and tomato paste. Microwave at High for 3½ to 5 minutes, or until mixture thickens and bubbles, stirring twice. Blend in sour cream. Add meatballs, turning to coat with sauce. Microwave at 50% (Medium) for 2 to 4 minutes, or until hot. Sprinkle with parsley. Serve with egg noodles.

Serving suggestion: Spoon meatballs and sauce into lettuce-lined pita loaves or serve open-face on hoagie buns.

Per Serving: Calories: 430 • Protein: 28 g. • Carbohydrate: 32 g. • Fat: 20 g.
• Cholesterol: 157 mg. • Sodium: 420 mg.
Exchanges: 2 starch, 3 medium-fat meat, ½ vegetable, 1 fat

North African Meatballs

Meatballs:
- 1 lb. lean ground beef, crumbled
- 1 egg
- 1/4 teaspoon celery seed
- 1/4 teaspoon ground cumin
- 1/4 teaspoon ground cinnamon
- 1/4 teaspoon garlic powder
- 1/8 teaspoon cayenne

- 1 can (14 1/2 oz.) Roma tomatoes, undrained and cut up
- 1 pkg. (0.87 oz.) brown gravy mix
- 1 medium zucchini, cut lengthwise into quarters and then crosswise into 1 1/2-inch chunks
- 1 small onion, cut into 8 wedges
- 1 can (23 oz.) sweet potatoes, drained and cut into 1-inch lengths

4 servings

In medium mixing bowl, combine all meatball ingredients. Shape into 16 meatballs, about 1 1/2 inches in diameter. Arrange in even layer in 8-inch square baking dish. Microwave at High for 6 to 8 minutes, or until meatballs are firm and no longer pink, rearranging once. Drain. Set aside.

In 2-quart casserole, combine tomatoes and brown gravy mix. Stir to dissolve gravy mix. Add zucchini, onion and meatballs. Mix well. Cover. Microwave at High for 8 to 10 minutes, or until zucchini is tender, stirring twice. Add sweet potatoes. Stir gently to coat. Let stand, covered, for 5 minutes, or until sweet potatoes are hot. Serve over hot cooked couscous or rice, if desired.

Per Serving: Calories: 400 • Protein: 25 g.
• Carbohydrate: 37 g. • Fat: 17 g.
• Cholesterol: 124 mg. • Sodium: 590 mg.
Exchanges: 1 1/2 starch, 2 medium-fat meat, 3 vegetable, 1 fat

Cheesy Baked Sloppy Joes ▲

Meat Mixture:
- 1 lb. lean ground beef, crumbled
- 1/3 cup chopped onion
- 1/3 cup chopped green pepper
- 1 can (8 oz.) tomato sauce
- 2 tablespoons tomato paste
- 1 tablespoon packed brown sugar
- 2 teaspoons chili powder
- 1 teaspoon white vinegar
- 1/4 teaspoon salt

- 6 hamburger buns, split and toasted
  Prepared mustard
- 1 cup shredded Cheddar cheese

6 servings

Heat conventional oven to 350°F. In 2-quart casserole, combine ground beef, onion and green pepper. Microwave at High for 4 to 7 minutes, or until meat is no longer pink, stirring twice to break apart. Drain. Add remaining meat mixture ingredients. Mix well. Microwave at High for 5 to 6 minutes, or until mixture is hot and slightly thickened, stirring once or twice. Set aside.

Spread buns evenly with mustard. Arrange bottom halves of buns on foil-lined baking sheet. Top evenly with meat mixture. Sprinkle evenly with cheese. Add tops of buns. Cover with foil, sealing edges. Bake for 30 to 35 minutes, or until sloppy joes are hot and cheese is melted.

Per Serving: Calories: 380 • Protein: 22 g. • Carbohydrate: 30 g. • Fat: 19 g.
• Cholesterol: 69 mg. • Sodium: 790 mg.
Exchanges: 1 starch, 2 medium-fat meat, 3 vegetable, 1 1/2 fat

Start with a basic meat filling and make three vegetable dishes, each with its own distinctive character.

Meat Filling

1 lb. lean ground beef, crumbled
½ cup seasoned dry bread crumbs
½ cup frozen corn
⅓ cup finely chopped green or red pepper
1 egg

How to Make Meat Filling

Combine all ingredients in medium mixing bowl. Season as directed in recipes opposite.

Zucchini Italiano*

1 recipe Meat Filling (left)
1 teaspoon dried oregano leaves
4 medium zucchini (6 to 8 oz. each)
1 can (14½ oz.) diced tomatoes, drained
⅓ cup shredded fresh Parmesan cheese

4 to 6 servings

Prepare meat filling as directed, adding oregano. Set aside. Remove thin slice from top of each zucchini. Scoop out center pulp and seeds, leaving ¼-inch shell. Discard pulp and seeds.

Divide meat filling mixture into quarters. Stuff one-fourth of mixture into each zucchini. Arrange stuffed zucchini in 8-inch square baking dish. Top evenly with tomatoes. Cover with wax paper or microwave cooking paper. Microwave at High for 14 to 15 minutes, or until meat mixture is firm and no longer pink, rotating dish twice and rearranging zucchini once.

Sprinkle evenly with Parmesan cheese. Microwave at High, uncovered, for 1 to 1½ minutes, or until cheese is melted. Re-cover. Let stand for 5 minutes.

*Recipe not recommended for ovens with less than 600 cooking watts.

Per Serving: Calories: 260 • Protein: 20 g. • Carbohydrate: 16 g. • Fat: 13 g.
• Cholesterol: 87 mg. • Sodium: 230 mg.
Exchanges: 2 medium-fat meat, 3 vegetable, ½ fat

Savory-stuffed Eggplant*

1 recipe Meat Filling
  (opposite)
1 teaspoon Italian seasoning
1 eggplant (about 1½ lbs.)

Sauce:
1 can (8 oz.) tomato sauce
1 tablespoon olive oil
¼ teaspoon Italian seasoning
¼ teaspoon sugar

½ cup shredded fresh
  Parmesan cheese (optional)

6 servings

Prepare meat filling as directed, adding 1 teaspoon Italian seasoning. Set aside. Remove thin slice from side of eggplant. Scoop out center pulp and seeds, leaving ¼-inch shell. Add 1 cup chopped pulp and seeds to meat filling mixture. Mix well. Stuff mixture into eggplant. Set aside.

In 8-inch square baking dish, combine all sauce ingredients. Place stuffed eggplant in dish. Cover with plastic wrap. Microwave at High for 15 to 22 minutes, or until meat mixture is firm and no longer pink and internal temperature registers 150°F. Spoon sauce over eggplant. Sprinkle evenly with Parmesan cheese.

Microwave at High for 1½ to 2 minutes, or until cheese is melted. Let stand for 5 minutes. Serve in slices.

*Recipe not recommended for ovens with less than 600 cooking watts.

Per Serving: Calories: 270 • Protein: 18 g.
• Carbohydrate: 20 g. • Fat: 14 g.
• Cholesterol: 83 mg. • Sodium: 360 mg.
Exchanges: ½ starch, 2 medium-fat meat, 2½ vegetable, ½ fat

New Mexican Baked Tomatoes*▲

1 recipe Meat Filling
  (opposite)
2 teaspoons chili powder
¼ to ½ teaspoon garlic powder

4 large, firm tomatoes (about
  10 oz. each)
½ cup shredded Monterey
  Jack cheese

4 servings

Prepare meat filling as directed, adding chili powder and garlic powder. Set aside. Remove thin slice from top of each tomato. Scoop out center pulp and seeds, leaving ¼-inch shell. (Save pulp for future use.) Place tomatoes cut-sides-down on paper-towel-lined plate to drain. Divide meat filling mixture into quarters. Stuff one-fourth of mixture into each tomato.

Arrange stuffed tomatoes in 8-inch square baking dish. Cover with wax paper or microwave cooking paper. Microwave at High for 10 to 14 minutes, or until meat mixture is firm and no longer pink, rotating dish and turning tomatoes twice. Sprinkle evenly with cheese. Microwave at High, uncovered, for 1 to 1½ minutes, or until cheese is melted. Re-cover. Let stand for 5 minutes.

*Recipe not recommended for ovens with less than 600 cooking watts.

Per Serving: Calories: 410 • Protein: 29 g. • Carbohydrate: 25 g. • Fat: 22 g.
• Cholesterol: 136 mg. • Sodium: 280 mg.
Exchanges: ½ starch, 3 medium-fat meat, 3½ vegetable, 1½ fat

Deep-dish Spaghetti Pie

Crust:

- 8 oz. uncooked spaghetti
- 1 egg
- ¼ cup grated Parmesan cheese
- 1 tablespoon all-purpose flour

Cheese Filling:

- 1 cup ricotta cheese
- 1 egg
- 1 tablespoon all-purpose flour
- 1 tablespoon dried parsley flakes

Meat Mixture:

- 1 lb. lean ground beef, crumbled
- 1⅔ cups spaghetti sauce, divided
- ½ teaspoon Italian seasoning

6 to 8 servings

Per Serving: Calories: 350 • Protein: 21 g.
• Carbohydrate: 33 g. • Fat: 15 g.
• Cholesterol: 100 mg. • Sodium: 400 mg.
Exchanges: 1½ starch, 2 medium-fat meat, 2 vegetable, 1 fat

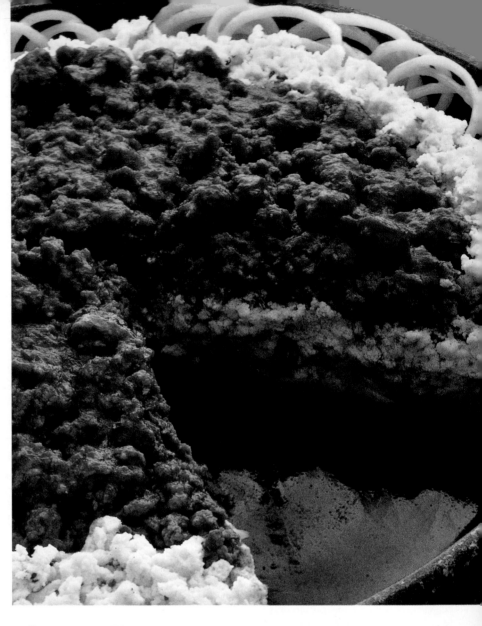

How to Microwave Deep-dish Spaghetti Pie

Prepare spaghetti as directed on package. Rinse and drain. In small mixing bowl, combine remaining crust ingredients. Add to spaghetti. Toss to coat evenly with egg mixture.

Spread spaghetti mixture over bottom and up sides of 10-inch deep-dish pie plate. Cover with plastic wrap. Microwave at 50% (Medium) for 5 to 7 minutes, or until set, rotating dish every 2 minutes. Set aside.

Combine cheese filling ingredients in medium mixing bowl. Microwave at 50% (Medium) for 4 to 6 minutes, or until mixture begins to stiffen, stirring after first 2 minutes and then every minute. Spread mixture over pasta crust. Set aside.

Place ground beef in 2-quart casserole. Microwave at High for 4 to 7 minutes, or until meat is no longer pink, stirring twice to break apart. Drain. Add ⅔ cup spaghetti sauce and the Italian seasoning. Mix well.

Spoon meat mixture evenly over cheese filling. Cover with plastic wrap. Microwave at 50% (Medium) for 7 to 10 minutes, or until temperature in center registers 140°F. Let stand, covered, for 5 minutes.

Place remaining 1 cup spaghetti sauce in medium mixing bowl. Microwave at High for 2½ to 4 minutes, or until hot. Serve pie in wedges. Spoon the sauce over each serving. Sprinkle with grated Parmesan cheese, if desired.

Easy Beef Tamales*

- 4 oz. cream cheese
- ¼ cup margarine or butter
- 2 eggs, slightly beaten
- 2 tablespoons honey
- 2 tablespoons milk
- 1¼ cups yellow cornmeal
- 1 teaspoon baking powder
- ¼ teaspoon salt
- ½ lb. lean ground beef, crumbled
- 1 can (16 oz.) whole tomatoes, drained and chopped, divided
- ¼ cup catsup

- 1 can (4 oz.) chopped green chilies, drained, divided
- 2 teaspoons chili powder
- 1 teaspoon ground cumin
- 1 can (10 oz.) enchilada sauce

4 servings

*Recipe not recommended for ovens with less than 600 cooking watts.

Per Serving: Calories: 600 • Protein: 20 g. • Carbohydrate: 57 g.
• Fat: 34 g. • Cholesterol: 173 mg. • Sodium: 1210 mg.
Exchanges: 2 starch, 1 medium-fat meat, 5½ vegetable, 5½ fat

How to Microwave Easy Beef Tamales

Cut eight 6-inch square pieces microwave cooking paper. Set aside. In small bowl, microwave cream cheese at High for 30 to 45 seconds, or until softened.

Place margarine in medium mixing bowl. Microwave at High for 1¼ to 1½ minutes, or until melted. Add cheese, eggs, honey and milk. Stir until smooth. Stir in cornmeal, baking powder and salt. Mix well. Cover with plastic wrap. Set batter aside.

Microwave ground beef in 2-quart casserole at High for 2 to 4 minutes, or until meat is no longer pink, stirring once to break apart. Drain. Add ⅓ cup tomatoes, the catsup, 2 tablespoons green chilies, the chili powder and cumin. Mix well.

Spread ¼ cup batter on 1 piece microwave cooking paper to 5 × 4-inch rectangle. Spoon a scant ¼ cup meat mixture down center of batter. Pull ends of paper up until dough meets, enclosing filling.

Roll up and arrange 4 tamales seam-sides-down around edges of 10-inch square casserole. Cover. Microwave at 70% (Medium High) for 5 to 6 minutes, or until tamales are firm, rotating dish twice. Remove from dish. Cover to keep warm.

Repeat with remaining tamales. In 4-cup measure, combine enchilada sauce, remaining tomatoes and green chilies. Microwave at High for 3 to 4 minutes, or until hot, stirring once. Remove paper from tamales. Spoon sauce over tamales.

Crunchy Chinatown Casserole

1 lb. lean ground beef, crumbled
1 pkg. (6 oz.) frozen pea pods
1 can (10¾ oz.) condensed cream of celery soup
1½ cups uncooked instant rice
1 cup ready-to-serve chicken broth
1 tablespoon soy sauce
1 cup diagonally sliced celery (½-inch slices)
½ cup thin red pepper strips
1 tablespoon water
1 cup chow mein noodles

4 to 6 servings

In 2-quart casserole, microwave ground beef at High for 4 to 7 minutes, or until meat is no longer pink, stirring twice to break apart. Drain. Add pea pods, soup, rice, broth and soy sauce. Set aside.

In small mixing bowl, combine celery, pepper strips and water. Cover with plastic wrap. Microwave at High for 2 to 4 minutes, or until vegetables are tender-crisp, stirring once. Drain. Add to ground beef mixture. Mix well. Cover. Microwave at High for 10 to 13 minutes, or until mixture is hot, stirring twice. Sprinkle with chow mein noodles. Microwave at High, uncovered, for 2 to 3 minutes, or until hot.

Per Serving: Calories: 340 • Protein: 18 g. • Carbohydrate: 32 g. • Fat: 15 g.
• Cholesterol: 52 mg. • Sodium: 780 mg.
Exchanges: 1½ starch, 1½ medium-fat meat, 2 vegetable, 1 fat

Cottage Chili Casserole

Topping:

- 1 container (12 oz.) small-curd cottage cheese
- 1 cup shredded Cheddar cheese
- 1 tablespoon dried parsley flakes

- 1 pkg. (12 oz.) uncooked mini lasagna noodles
- 1 lb. lean ground beef, crumbled
- 1 can (15 oz.) chili beans in chili sauce
- 1 can (14½ oz.) diced tomatoes, undrained
- 1 can (6 oz.) tomato paste
- ½ cup chopped green pepper
- 2 teaspoons chili powder
- 1 teaspoon sugar

6 to 8 servings

In small mixing bowl, combine all topping ingredients. Set aside. Prepare noodles as directed on package. Rinse and drain. Set aside.

In 3-quart casserole, microwave ground beef at High for 4 to 7 minutes, or until meat is no longer pink, stirring twice to break apart. Drain. Add noodles and remaining ingredients, except topping. Mix well. Cover. Microwave at High for 5 to 9 minutes, or until mixture is hot, stirring twice. Spread topping evenly over meat mixture. Microwave at High for 5 to 7 minutes, or until topping is hot and melted, rotating twice.

Per Serving: Calories: 470 • Protein: 30 g. • Carbohydrate: 48 g. • Fat: 19 g. • Cholesterol: 109 mg. • Sodium: 840 mg. Exchanges: 2½ starch, 2½ lean meat, 2 vegetable, 2 fat

Variation:
Cottage Lasagna Casserole: Prepare recipe as directed, except substitute mozzarella cheese for Cheddar cheese, 1 can (15 oz.) tomato sauce for chili beans and 1 teaspoon Italian seasoning for chili powder.

Beef & Wild Rice Bake

1 pkg. (6 oz.) long-grain white and wild rice mix
⅓ cup unseasoned dry bread crumbs
1 lb. lean ground beef, crumbled
½ cup chopped onion
1 can (5 oz.) evaporated milk
2 eggs
¼ cup plus 3 tablespoons all-purpose flour, divided
⅓ cup slivered almonds
1 cup sliced fresh mushrooms
2 tablespoons margarine or butter
¼ teaspoon salt
¼ teaspoon pepper
1 cup ready-to-serve beef broth
1 tablespoon sherry
¼ cup sliced green onions

6 servings

Lightly grease 8-inch square baking dish. Set aside. Prepare rice conventionally as directed on package, except reduce water to 2 cups. Add bread crumbs to cooked rice. Mix well. Set aside. In 2-quart casserole, combine ground beef and onion. Microwave at High for 6 to 7 minutes, or until meat is no longer pink and onion is tender, stirring twice to break apart. Drain. Add rice mixture to ground beef mixture. Set aside.

In small mixing bowl, blend milk, eggs and ¼ cup flour. Add milk mixture and almonds to ground beef and rice mixture. Mix well. Press mixture into prepared baking dish. Cover with plastic wrap. Microwave at 50% (Medium) for 10 to 12 minutes, or until center is set, rotating dish every 3 minutes. Let stand, covered, for 5 minutes.

In 4-cup measure, combine mushrooms and margarine. Microwave at High for 3 to 4 minutes, or until mushrooms are tender, stirring once. Stir in remaining 3 tablespoons flour, the salt and pepper. Blend in broth and sherry. Add green onions. Microwave at High for 5 to 8 minutes, or until sauce thickens and bubbles, stirring 2 or 3 times. Cut wild rice bake into squares. Spoon sauce over each serving.

Per Serving: Calories: 460 • Protein: 23 g. • Carbohydrate: 41 g. • Fat: 22 g.
• Cholesterol: 125 mg. • Sodium: 400 mg.
Exchanges: 2 starch, 2 medium-fat meat, 2 vegetable, 2 fat

Meat-stuffed Focaccia Loaf

Olive oil
1 loaf (16 oz.) frozen white bread dough, defrosted*

Meat Mixture:

½ lb. lean ground beef, crumbled
⅓ cup chopped onion
¼ cup sliced pimiento-stuffed green olives
¼ cup catsup
½ teaspoon Italian seasoning
¼ teaspoon crushed red pepper flakes

½ cup shredded mozzarella or Monterey Jack cheese
Olive oil
1 clove garlic, minced
½ teaspoon Italian seasoning

4 servings

*To microwave-defrost bread dough, wrap loaf in greased sheet of wax paper or microwave cooking paper. Twist ends to seal. Microwave at 50% (Medium) for 2 minutes. Let stand for 5 minutes. Turn over. Microwave at 50% (Medium) for 1 to 2 minutes, or until soft to the touch. Dough should remain cool.

Per Serving: Calories: 500 • Protein: 23 g. • Carbohydrate: 61 g. • Fat: 18 g. • Cholesterol: 48 mg. • Sodium: 1060 mg.
Exchanges: 3½ starch, 1½ medium-fat meat, 2 vegetable, ½ fat

How to Make Meat-stuffed Focaccia Loaf

Brush large baking sheet with oil. Set aside. Divide dough in half. Stretch one half into 10-inch circle. Place on prepared baking sheet. Set aside. In 2-quart casserole, microwave ground beef at High for 2 to 4 minutes, or until meat is no longer pink, stirring once to break apart. Drain. Add remaining meat mixture ingredients. Mix well.

Spoon mixture onto bread dough circle, spreading to within 1 inch of edge. Sprinkle with cheese. Stretch remaining dough into 10-inch circle. Fit over filling, pressing edges together to seal. Cover with cloth and let rise in warm place about 45 minutes. Test dough by pressing 2 fingers about ½ inch into dough; impressions should remain.

Heat conventional oven to 350°F. Using fingertips, make indentations randomly over surface of dough. Brush lightly with oil. Sprinkle with garlic and ½ teaspoon Italian seasoning. Bake for 25 to 30 minutes, or until golden brown. Serve in wedges.

Spicy Beef & Phyllo Pie

Meat Mixture:

- 1 lb. lean ground beef, crumbled
- 2 tablespoons all-purpose flour
- 2 tablespoons dried parsley flakes
- 1/2 teaspoon garlic powder
- 1/2 teaspoon crushed red pepper flakes
- 1/4 teaspoon pepper
- 1/4 teaspoon salt

Vegetable Mixture:

- 1 cup julienne red and green peppers (2 × 1/4-inch strips)
- 1 can (4 oz.) mushroom stems and pieces, drained
- 1/2 cup ricotta cheese
- 16 sheets frozen phyllo dough (18 × 14-inch sheets), defrosted
- 1/4 cup margarine or butter

6 servings

In 2-quart casserole, combine all meat mixture ingredients. Microwave at High for 5 to 8 minutes, or until meat is no longer pink, stirring twice to break apart. Set aside. In 1-quart casserole, combine pepper strips and mushrooms. Cover. Microwave at High for 4 to 6 minutes, or until peppers are tender, stirring once or twice. Drain. Cool slightly. Add ricotta cheese. Mix well. Set aside.

Heat conventional oven to 350°F. Place 2 pieces of plastic wrap (12 × 20-inch) side by side on flat work surface. Remove phyllo sheets from package and unroll on prepared work surface. Cover with plastic wrap. In 2-cup measure, microwave margarine at High for 1 1/4 to 1 1/2 minutes, or until melted. Brush bottom and sides of 8-inch square baking dish lightly with melted margarine. Remove 1 sheet phyllo. Fold in half crosswise and then lengthwise to fit dish. Place in prepared dish. Brush lightly with melted margarine. Repeat with 3 more sheets. Spread half of meat mixture over phyllo.

Repeat layering phyllo and brushing with margarine, using 4 more sheets. Spread vegetable mixture evenly over phyllo. Repeat layering phyllo and brushing with margarine, using 4 more sheets. Spread remaining meat mixture over phyllo. Repeat layering phyllo and brushing with margarine, using remaining phyllo sheets. Using sharp knife, score top of pie in diamond pattern. Bake for 35 to 40 minutes, or until puffed and golden brown. Serve in squares.

Per Serving: Calories: 330 • Protein: 18 g. • Carbohydrate: 19 g. • Fat: 20 g.
• Cholesterol: 55 mg. • Sodium: 470 mg.
Exchanges: 1 starch, 2 medium-fat meat, 1 vegetable, 2 fat

Start with One Pound of Boneless Beef Sirloin

By using strips of well-trimmed boneless beef sirloin you can serve a main dish of tender, flavorful steak that is both economical and low in fat. To make slicing easy, partially freeze the beef before cutting it into strips. For even greater economy, substitute boneless top round. The meat will be less tender than steak, but cutting it into strips helps tenderize it.

Garlic Steak Strips

1 tablespoon vegetable oil
1-lb. boneless beef sirloin steak, about ¾ inch thick, cut into thin strips
2 cloves garlic, minced

How to Make Garlic Steak Strips

Heat vegetable oil conventionally over medium-high heat in 10-inch skillet.

Add beef strips and garlic. Sauté for 4 to 5 minutes, or until meat is lightly browned. Remove from heat.

◄ Steak Sukiyaki

1 recipe Garlic Steak Strips (left)
1 tablespoon plus 1 teaspoon cornstarch
2 tablespoons sugar
½ cup water
⅓ cup soy sauce
2 cups red and green julienne peppers (2 × ¼-inch strips)
1 cup sliced fresh mushrooms
¼ cup thinly sliced carrot
¼ cup sliced green onions

4 servings

Prepare steak strips as directed. Set aside. In 2-quart casserole, combine cornstarch and sugar. Blend in water and soy sauce. Add remaining ingredients. Mix well.

Microwave at High, uncovered, for 7 to 11 minutes, or until mixture is thickened and translucent and vegetables are tender-crisp, stirring 2 or 3 times. Add steak strips. Mix well. Microwave at High for 2 to 4 minutes, or until hot. Serve over hot cooked rice, if desired.

Per Serving: Calories: 260 • Protein: 25 g. • Carbohydrate: 18 g. • Fat: 10 g. • Cholesterol: 66 mg. • Sodium: 1440 mg. Exchanges: 2½ lean meat, 3½ vegetable, ½ fat

Steak Pizzola

1 recipe Garlic Steak Strips (left)
1 can (16 oz.) whole tomatoes, drained and cut up
1 jar (14 oz.) pizza sauce
1 can (4.5 oz.) sliced mushrooms, drained
½ cup chopped green pepper
2 teaspoons sugar
½ teaspoon dried basil leaves
½ teaspoon dried oregano leaves

4 servings

Prepare steak strips as directed. Set aside. In 2-quart casserole, combine remaining ingredients. Microwave at High, uncovered, for 5 to 8 minutes, or until sauce is hot and slightly thickened, stirring once or twice. Add steak strips. Mix well.

Microwave at High for 4 to 5 minutes, or until hot, stirring once. Serve over toasted French bread or hot cooked rice, if desired.

Per Serving: Calories: 290 • Protein: 25 g. • Carbohydrate: 20 g. • Fat: 12 g. • Cholesterol: 65 mg. • Sodium: 730 mg. Exchanges: 2½ lean meat, 4 vegetable, 1 fat

Steak Teriyaki

1 recipe Garlic Steak Strips
  (page 23)
1 pkg. (6 oz.) frozen pea
  pods
2 tablespoons cornstarch
1 tablespoon sugar
1/4 teaspoon ground ginger
1/2 cup water
1/3 cup teriyaki sauce
1/2 cup julienne carrot
  (2 × 1/4-inch strips)
1/2 cup sliced fresh mushrooms
1 can (8 oz.) whole water
  chestnuts, rinsed and
  drained

4 servings

Prepare steak strips as directed.
Set aside. Remove pea pods
from packaging. Place on plate.
Microwave at High for 2 to 3
minutes, or until defrosted, stirring once to break apart. Drain.
Set aside.

In 2-quart casserole, combine
cornstarch, sugar and ginger.
Blend in water and teriyaki
sauce. Add carrot, mushrooms
and water chestnuts. Mix well.
Microwave at High, uncovered,
for 7 to 8 minutes, or until mixture
is thickened and translucent and
vegetables are tender-crisp,
stirring 2 or 3 times.

Add steak strips and pea pods.
Mix well. Microwave at High for
2 to 3 minutes, or until hot. Serve
over hot cooked fettucini or rice,
if desired.

Per Serving: Calories: 296 • Protein: 26 g.
• Carbohydrate: 25 g. • Fat: 10 g.
• Cholesterol: 66 mg. • Sodium: 983 mg.
Exchanges: 1 starch, 3 lean meat,
2 vegetable

Sweet & Sour Beef ▲

1 recipe Garlic Steak Strips
  (page 23)
2 tablespoons packed brown
  sugar
1 tablespoon plus 1 teaspoon
  cornstarch
1/3 cup water
1/3 cup soy sauce
2 tablespoons white vinegar

1 cup green pepper chunks
  (3/4-inch)
1 cup thinly sliced carrot
  strips
1 can (8 oz.) pineapple chunks
  in juice, drained, or 1 cup
  fresh pineapple chunks
1/4 cup sliced green onions

4 servings

Prepare steak strips as directed. Set aside. In 2-quart casserole,
combine sugar and cornstarch. Blend in water, soy sauce and
vinegar. Add remaining ingredients. Mix well.

Microwave at High, uncovered, for 7 to 12 minutes, or until mixture is
thickened and translucent and vegetables are tender-crisp, stirring
2 or 3 times. Add steak strips. Mix well. Microwave at High for 2
to 4 minutes, or until hot. Serve over hot cooked rice or spaghetti,
if desired.

Per Serving: Calories: 280 • Protein: 25 g. • Carbohydrate: 23 g. • Fat: 10 g.
• Cholesterol: 65 mg. • Sodium: 1450 mg.
Exchanges: 3 lean meat, 1 1/2 vegetable, 1 fruit

24

Steak & Potato Stir-fry

4 to 5 new potatoes
 (about 1 lb.)
1 cup fresh green beans,
 trimmed and sliced
 lengthwise
¼ cup water
3 tablespoons vegetable oil,
 divided
¼ teaspoon plus ⅛ teaspoon
 garlic powder, divided
2 teaspoons cornstarch
¾ cup ready-to-serve beef
 broth
1 tablespoon Worcestershire
 sauce
1- lb. boneless beef sirloin
 steak, about ¾ inch thick,
 cut into thin strips
⅓ cup coarsely chopped red
 pepper

6 servings

In 2-quart casserole, place potatoes, green beans and water. Cover. Microwave at High for 6 to 7 minutes, or until potatoes are tender-crisp, stirring once. Let stand, covered, for 5 minutes. Drain. Slice potatoes into ¼-inch slices. Add 1 tablespoon oil and ¼ teaspoon garlic powder to potatoes and beans. Toss gently to coat. Set aside. Place cornstarch in small mixing bowl. Blend in broth and Worcestershire sauce. Set aside.

In 10-inch skillet, heat remaining 2 tablespoons oil and ⅛ teaspoon garlic powder conventionally over medium-high heat until hot. Add steak strips. Sauté for 4 to 5 minutes, or until meat is lightly browned. Add red pepper. Sauté for 3 to 4 minutes, or until tender. Add potatoes and beans mixture and sauce to skillet. Cook for 2 to 3 minutes longer, or until mixture thickens and bubbles, stirring gently 2 or 3 times. Serve over hot cooked fettucini or egg noodles, if desired.

Per Serving: Calories: 200 • Protein: 18 g. • Carbohydrate: 18 g. • Fat: 7 g.
• Cholesterol: 44 mg. • Sodium: 160 mg.
Exchanges: 1 starch, 2 lean meat, ½ vegetable

Parisienne Beef

8 oz. sliced fresh mushrooms
   (about 3 cups)
2 tablespoons margarine or
   butter
1-lb. boneless beef sirloin
   steak, about ¾ inch thick,
   cut into thin strips
¼ teaspoon onion salt
2 teaspoons cornstarch
¼ teaspoon salt
2 cans (5 oz. each)
   evaporated milk or 1¼
   cups half-and-half
2 tablespoons dry sherry
1 tablespoon white wine
   Worcestershire sauce

4 servings

In 2-quart casserole, place mushrooms and margarine. Cover. Microwave at High for 3 to 4 minutes, or until tender, stirring once. Set aside. In 1-quart casserole, combine beef strips and onion salt. Microwave at High for 6 to 7 minutes, or until meat is no longer pink, stirring once. Drain. Set aside.

Stir cornstarch and salt into mushrooms and margarine. Blend in milk, sherry and Worcestershire sauce. Mix well. Add beef strips. Mix well. Cover. Microwave at High for 10 to 11 minutes, or until mixture thickens and bubbles, stirring gently every 2 minutes. Serve over hot cooked noodles or rice, if desired.

Per Serving: Calories: 340 • Protein: 29 g. • Carbohydrate: 13 g. • Fat: 18 g.
• Cholesterol: 88 mg. • Sodium: 470 mg.
Exchanges: 3 lean meat, 1½ vegetable, ½ low-fat milk, 1½ fat

Variation:

Parisienne Beef Potatoes: Bake 4 large baking potatoes (8 to 10 oz. each) as directed on page 147. Set aside. Unwrap 1 package (10 oz.) frozen baby carrots. Place on plate. Microwave at High for 4 to 6 minutes, or until defrosted, stirring once to break apart. Drain. Set aside. Prepare recipe as directed, except increase cornstarch to 1 tablespoon and add carrots to sauce before microwaving. Place potatoes on serving plates. Split open. Spoon mixture evenly over potatoes.

Salsa Beef with Green Chili Potato Pancakes

    2 tablespoons margarine or
        butter
    1 cup water
    ½ cup milk
    ½ cup frozen corn
    3 tablespoons canned
        chopped green chilies,
        drained
    1 jar (2 oz.) diced pimiento,
        drained
    ⅛ teaspoon cayenne
  2½ cups instant mashed
        potato flakes
    2 to 3 tablespoons
        all-purpose flour
        Vegetable oil
  1-lb. boneless beef sirloin
        steak, about ¾ inch thick,
        cut into thin strips
    ¼ teaspoon garlic powder
  1½ cups salsa

                    6 servings

Per Serving: Calories: 350 • Protein: 18 g.
• Carbohydrate: 28 g. • Fat: 18 g.
• Cholesterol: 45 mg. • Sodium: 640 mg.
Exchanges: 1 starch, 1½ lean meat,
2½ vegetable, 2½ fat

How to Make Salsa Beef with Green Chili Potato Pancakes

Microwave margarine in 2-quart casserole at High for 45 seconds to 1 minute, or until melted. Add water, milk, corn, chilies, pimiento and cayenne. Mix well. Add potato flakes. Mix well. (Mixture will be stiff.) Divide mixture into 6 equal portions. Shape each portion into 3½-inch patty.

Sprinkle flour on sheet of wax paper or microwave cooking paper. Dredge both sides of each patty in flour. In 10-inch skillet, heat ⅛ inch oil conventionally over medium heat. Fry patties for 4 to 5 minutes on each side, or until golden brown. Place patties on serving platter. Cover to keep warm.

Place beef strips in 1-quart casserole. Sprinkle with garlic powder. Microwave at High for 6 to 7 minutes, or until meat is no longer pink, stirring twice. Drain. Add salsa. Mix well. Cover. Microwave at High for 2 to 3 minutes, or until hot, stirring once. Spoon beef mixture over pancakes. Garnish with sliced green onion or snipped fresh parsley, if desired.

Tortilla roll-ups, brushed lightly with oil and baked crisp in a conventional oven, absorb far less fat than traditionally fried chimichangas.

Pepper Steak Tortilla Pockets

Vegetable oil
1 cup chopped green and red peppers
½ cup sliced green onions
1 clove garlic, minced
1 tablespoon margarine or butter

2 teaspoons cornstarch
1-lb. boneless beef sirloin steak, about ¾ inch thick, cut into thin strips
¼ cup steak sauce
¼ cup catsup

6 flour tortillas (10-inch)

6 servings

Per Serving: Calories: 290 • Protein: 19 g. • Carbohydrate: 33 g. • Fat: 10 g. • Cholesterol: 44 mg. • Sodium: 680 mg. Exchanges: 1 starch, 1½ lean meat, 3½ vegetable, 1 fat

How to Make Pepper Steak Tortilla Pockets

Brush large baking sheet with oil. Set aside. Heat conventional oven to 450°F. In 2-quart casserole, combine green and red peppers, onions, garlic and margarine. Cover.

Microwave at High for 3 to 6 minutes, or until vegetables are tender, stirring once. Sprinkle cornstarch over vegetables. Mix well.

Add beef strips, steak sauce and catsup. Mix well. Microwave at High, uncovered, for 5 to 7 minutes, or until meat is no longer pink and sauce is thickened, stirring 2 or 3 times. Cool slightly.

Spoon ½ cup meat mixture across bottom half of 1 tortilla, to within 1½ inches of sides. Fold up tortilla just until meat mixture is enclosed. Fold in sides. Roll up tortilla.

Secure with wooden pick. Place on prepared baking sheet. Brush lightly with oil. Repeat with remaining meat mixture and tortillas.

Bake for 12 to 15 minutes, or until light golden brown. Top with sour cream and additional sliced green onion, if desired.

Broccoli, Beef & Cheese Tortilla Pockets

Vegetable oil
½ cup chopped red pepper
½ cup sliced green onions
1 cup frozen chopped broccoli
1 clove garlic, minced
1 tablespoon margarine or butter
1 - lb. boneless beef sirloin steak, about ¾ inch thick, cut into thin strips
6 flour tortillas (10-inch)
1½ cups shredded Monterey Jack cheese

6 servings

Brush large baking sheet with oil. Set aside. Heat conventional oven to 450°F. In 2-quart casserole, combine red pepper, onions, broccoli, garlic and margarine. Cover. Microwave at High for 5 to 6 minutes, or until vegetables are tender, stirring once. Set aside. In 1-quart casserole, microwave beef strips at High for 6 to 7 minutes, or until meat is no longer pink, stirring twice. Drain. Add beef strips to vegetable mixture. Mix well.

Spoon ½ cup meat mixture across bottom half of 1 tortilla, to within 1½ inches of sides. Sprinkle with 2 tablespoons cheese. Fold up tortilla just until meat mixture is enclosed. Fold in sides. Roll up tortilla. Secure with wooden pick. Place on prepared baking sheet. Brush lightly with oil. Repeat with remaining meat mixture and tortillas. Bake for 12 to 15 minutes, or until light golden brown. Top with sour cream and additional sliced green onion, if desired.

Per Serving: Calories: 370 • Protein: 26 g. • Carbohydrate: 27 g. • Fat: 18 g.
• Cholesterol: 69 mg. • Sodium: 470 mg.
Exchanges: 1 starch, 2½ lean meat, 2½ vegetable, 2 fat

Start with Four Pork Chops

Create satisfying, homey meals with pork chops. In these easy, one-dish recipes, a vegetable accompaniment cooks with the chops to enhance and blend flavors.

Chili-spiced Pork Chops

    4 pork loin chops (5 to 6 oz. each), about
       ³⁄₄ inch thick
    1 can (16 oz.) whole tomatoes, cut up and
       undrained
    1 can (6 oz.) tomato paste
    1 teaspoon chili powder
  ¹⁄₂ teaspoon sugar
  ¹⁄₄ teaspoon salt
  ¹⁄₄ teaspoon ground cumin
  ¹⁄₈ teaspoon cayenne
    1 medium onion, cut into thin wedges
    1 cup thinly sliced carrots
  ¹⁄₄ cup raisins

4 servings

Arrange pork chops in 10-inch square casserole with meaty portions toward outside. Set aside. In medium mixing bowl, combine tomatoes, tomato paste, chili powder, sugar, salt, cumin and cayenne. Stir in remaining ingredients.

Spoon mixture evenly over pork chops. Cover. Microwave at High for 10 minutes. Microwave at 70% (Medium High) for 10 to 15 minutes longer, or until meat near bone is no longer pink, turning chops over once and stirring sauce once or twice. Serve with hot cooked rice, if desired.

Per Serving: Calories: 372 • Protein: 35 g. • Carbohydrate: 23 g. • Fat: 16 g. • Cholesterol: 89 mg. • Sodium: 560 mg. Exchanges: 3¹⁄₂ lean meat, 4¹⁄₂ vegetable, 1 fat

Variation:
◀ **Cacciatore Pork Chops:** Prepare recipe as directed, except substitute ¹⁄₂ teaspoon Italian seasoning for chili powder, ¹⁄₈ teaspoon garlic powder for cumin and 1 medium zucchini cut into 2 × ¹⁄₄-inch strips for raisins. Serve over hot cooked fettucini.

Creamy Basil Pork Chops & Potatoes

    4 pork loin chops (5 to 6 oz. each), about
       ³⁄₄ inch thick
    1 teaspoon dried basil leaves, divided
  ¹⁄₂ teaspoon paprika
  ¹⁄₂ teaspoon salt, divided
  ¹⁄₈ teaspoon cayenne
    4 cups cubed red potatoes (¹⁄₂-inch cubes)
  ¹⁄₂ cup chopped green pepper
    2 tablespoons all-purpose flour
 1¹⁄₂ cups milk
    1 cup shredded Cheddar or Swiss cheese

4 servings

Arrange pork chops in 10-inch square casserole with meaty portions toward outside. In small bowl, combine ¹⁄₂ teaspoon basil leaves, the paprika, ¹⁄₄ teaspoon salt and the cayenne. Sprinkle evenly over pork chops. Cover with wax paper or microwave cooking paper. Microwave at 70% (Medium High) for 12 to 17 minutes, or until meat near bone is no longer pink, turning chops over once. Remove pork chops from casserole. Set aside.

Drain casserole well. In same casserole, combine potatoes, green pepper, flour, the remaining ¹⁄₂ teaspoon basil leaves and ¹⁄₄ teaspoon salt. Pour milk over potato mixture. Cover. Microwave at High for 5 minutes. Stir. Re-cover. Microwave at 70% (Medium High) for 15 to 22 minutes, or until sauce thickens and potatoes are tender, stirring twice. Stir in ³⁄₄ cup cheese. Arrange pork chops over potatoes. Sprinkle with the remaining ¹⁄₄ cup cheese. Re-cover. Microwave at 70% (Medium High) for 5 to 10 minutes, or until cheese is melted.

Per Serving: Calories: 574 • Protein: 46 g. • Carbohydrate: 36 g. • Fat: 27 g. • Cholesterol: 126 mg. • Sodium: 549 mg. Exchanges: 1¹⁄₂ starch, 5 lean meat, 1¹⁄₂ vegetable, ¹⁄₂ low-fat milk, 2 fat

Pork Chops with Spiced Apple Salsa

2 tablespoons vegetable oil
1 teaspoon pumpkin pie spice, divided
4 pork loin chops (5 to 6 oz. each), about ¾ inch thick
⅓ cup packed brown sugar
1 teaspoon cornstarch
¼ teaspoon salt
1 tablespoon margarine or butter
⅓ cup orange juice
½ cup coarsely chopped walnuts
1 medium red apple, cored and coarsely chopped
1 medium green apple, cored and coarsely chopped

4 servings

In 10-inch skillet, heat oil conventionally over medium-high heat until hot. Add ½ teaspoon pumpkin pie spice. Stir. Add pork chops. Cook for 8 to 10 minutes, or until meat near bone is no longer pink, turning over once. Place chops in 10-inch square casserole. Cover. Set aside.

In 1½-quart casserole, combine sugar, cornstarch, remaining ½ teaspoon pumpkin pie spice, the salt and margarine. Blend in orange juice. Microwave at High, uncovered, for 2 to 2½ minutes, or until mixture is clear and translucent, stirring once. Add nuts and apples. Stir to coat.

Spoon salsa mixture evenly over pork chops. Cover. Microwave at 70% (Medium High) for 3 to 5 minutes, or until hot.

Per Serving: Calories: 581 • Protein: 34 g. • Carbohydrate: 34 g. • Fat: 35 g.
• Cholesterol: 89 mg. • Sodium: 227 mg.
Exchanges: 4½ lean meat, 2 fruit, 4½ fat

Chinese Pork Chops with Pineapple Fried Rice

Marinade:

- 3 tablespoons packed brown sugar
- 2 tablespoons soy sauce
- 2 tablespoons white wine
- 1/4 teaspoon ground ginger
- 1/4 teaspoon dry mustard

- 4 pork loin chops (5 to 6 oz. each), about 3/4 inch thick
- 1 1/2 cups uncooked instant rice
- 1 cup ready-to-serve chicken broth
- 1 can (8 oz.) pineapple tidbits, undrained
- 1/2 cup frozen peas
- 1/3 cup diagonally sliced green onions
- 1/4 cup chopped red pepper
- 2 teaspoons soy sauce
- 2 tablespoons vegetable oil

4 servings

In 8-inch square baking dish, combine all marinade ingredients. Stir to dissolve sugar. Arrange pork chops in dish, turning to coat. Cover with plastic wrap. Marinate chops in refrigerator at least 4 hours.

Drain and discard marinade. Set chops aside. In 10-inch square casserole, combine remaining ingredients, except oil. Set aside.

In 10-inch skillet, heat oil conventionally over medium-high heat until hot. Add pork chops. Cook about 5 minutes, or just until browned on both sides. Arrange chops over rice mixture. Cover. Microwave at 70% (Medium High) for 12 to 17 minutes, or until meat near bone is no longer pink and rice is tender, rotating dish and stirring rice twice. Let stand, covered, for 5 minutes.

Per Serving: Calories: 549 • Protein: 38 g. • Carbohydrate: 46 g. • Fat: 23 g.
• Cholesterol: 89 mg. • Sodium: 571 mg.
Exchanges: 2 starch, 4 1/2 lean meat, 1 fruit, 2 fat

Barbecued Pork Chops & Corn Casserole

- 1 tablespoon margarine or butter
- ¼ cup chopped red pepper
- ¼ cup sliced green onions
- 1 can (16½ oz.) cream-style corn
- 1 cup frozen corn
- 2 eggs
- ⅓ cup seasoned dry bread crumbs
- ¼ cup milk
- 2 tablespoons all-purpose flour
- ¼ teaspoon salt
- ½ envelope (3.5 oz.) barbecue-flavor seasoning and coating mix (about 6 tablespoons)
- 4 pork loin chops (5 to 6 oz. each), about ¾ inch thick
- 2 tablespoons vegetable oil

4 servings

In 10-inch square casserole, combine margarine, red pepper and onions. Cover. Microwave at High for 1½ to 2 minutes, or until margarine is melted and vegetables are tender. Add remaining ingredients, except coating mix, pork chops and oil. Mix well. Re-cover. Microwave at 70% (Medium High) for 10 minutes, stirring twice. Microwave at 70% (Medium High) for 2 to 3 minutes longer, or until center is set. Re-cover. Set aside.

Place coating mix in shallow dish. Dredge chops, coating both sides. In 10-inch skillet, heat oil conventionally over medium-high heat until hot. Add pork chops. Cook for 8 to 10 minutes, or until meat near bone is no longer pink, turning over once. Drain well. Arrange chops over corn mixture. Re-cover. Microwave at 70% (Medium High) for 3 to 5 minutes, or until hot.

Per Serving: Calories: 620 • Protein: 41 g. • Carbohydrate: 50 g. • Fat: 30 g. • Cholesterol: 197 mg. • Sodium: 1080 mg. Exchanges: 3 starch, 4 lean meat, 1 vegetable, 3 fat

Pan-fried Chops & Chunky Vegetables

3 tablespoons all-purpose
   flour
½ teaspoon onion powder
¼ teaspoon salt
4 pork loin chops (5 to 6 oz.
   each), about ¾ inch thick
2 tablespoons vegetable oil
2 tablespoons margarine or
   butter
4 medium carrots, cut into
   1-inch chunks (2 cups)
3 celery ribs, cut into 1-inch
   lengths
2 tablespoons Dijon mustard
1 tablespoon honey
1 teaspoon lemon juice
   Dash pepper
4 oz. fresh mushrooms,
   quartered (1 cup)

4 servings

In large plastic food-storage bag, combine flour, onion powder and salt. Add pork chops. Close bag. Shake to coat chops. In 10-inch skillet, heat oil conventionally over medium-high heat until hot. Add pork chops. Cook for 8 to 10 minutes, or until meat near bone is no longer pink, turning over once. Set aside.

In 10-inch square casserole, microwave margarine at High for 45 seconds to 1 minute, or until melted. Add carrots and celery. Cover. Microwave at High for 8 to 14 minutes, or until carrots and celery are tender-crisp.

In small bowl, combine mustard, honey, lemon juice and pepper. Add to vegetable mixture. Stir in mushrooms. Arrange chops in casserole. Spoon vegetable mixture over chops. Re-cover. Microwave at 70% (Medium High) for 8 to 11 minutes, or until vegetables are tender.

Per Serving: Calories: 478 • Protein: 34 g. • Carbohydrate: 19 g. • Fat: 29 g.
• Cholesterol: 89 mg. • Sodium: 526 mg.
Exchanges: ½ starch, 4 lean meat, 2 vegetable, 3½ fat

Pineapple Chutney Pork Chops

4 pork loin chops (5 to 6 oz.
    each), about ¾ inch thick
¼ cup soy sauce, divided
⅓ cup packed brown sugar
2 tablespoons cornstarch
¼ teaspoon ground cinnamon
¼ teaspoon ground ginger
1 can (20 oz.) pineapple
    tidbits in juice, drained
    (reserve ¾ cup juice)
⅓ cup cider vinegar
½ cup chopped dried apricots
½ cup chopped green pepper

4 servings

Arrange pork chops in 10-inch square casserole with meaty portions toward outside. Brush with 1 tablespoon soy sauce. Cover with wax paper or microwave cooking paper. Microwave at 70% (Medium High) for 12 to 17 minutes, or until meat near bone is no longer pink, turning chops over once. Drain. Set aside.

In medium mixing bowl, combine sugar, cornstarch, cinnamon and ginger. Blend in reserved pineapple juice, the vinegar and remaining 3 tablespoons soy sauce. Stir in pineapple tidbits and apricots. Microwave at High for 10 to 13 minutes, or until mixture is thickened and translucent, stirring once or twice. Stir in green pepper.

Spoon mixture over pork chops. Cover with wax paper or microwave cooking paper. Microwave at 70% (Medium High) for 12 to 16 minutes, or until pork chops are tender, turning chops over once and basting with sauce.

Per Serving: Calories: 503 • Protein: 34 g. • Carbohydrate: 58 g. • Fat: 16 g.
• Cholesterol: 89 mg. • Sodium: 1097 mg.
Exchanges: 4½ lean meat, 1 vegetable, 3½ fruit, ½ fat

Spicy Thai-style Pork & Noodles* ▶

2 cups uncooked fine egg
 noodles
4 boneless pork loin chops
 (4 to 6 oz. each), cut into
 thin strips
2 cloves garlic, minced
2 teaspoons sugar
¾ teaspoon ground ginger
½ teaspoon crushed red
 pepper flakes
2 cups fresh broccoli
 flowerets
1 cup fresh cauliflowerets
¾ cup ready-to-serve chicken
 broth
3 tablespoons soy sauce
2 tablespoons cornstarch
1 medium tomato, seeded
 and chopped
½ cup shredded carrot

6 servings

Prepare egg noodles as directed on package. Rinse and drain. Set aside. In 3-quart casserole, combine pork, garlic, sugar, ginger and red pepper flakes. Cover. Microwave at 70% (Medium High) for 6 to 8 minutes, or until meat is no longer pink, stirring once. Add broccoli, cauliflower and broth.

In small bowl, combine soy sauce and cornstarch. Add to pork mixture. Mix well. Cover. Microwave at 70% (Medium High) for 10 to 12 minutes, or until mixture is thickened and translucent and vegetables are tender, stirring twice. Add noodles, tomato and carrot. Mix well.

* Recipe not recommended for ovens with less than 600 cooking watts.

Per Serving: Calories: 300 • Protein: 28 g.
• Carbohydrate: 18 g. • Fat: 13 g.
• Cholesterol: 93 mg. • Sodium: 690 mg.
Exchanges: ½ starch, 3 lean meat,
2 vegetable, 1 fat

Sunshine Pork & Peppers

1 tablespoon cornstarch
½ teaspoon fennel seed,
 crushed
¼ teaspoon salt
½ cup orange juice
2 teaspoons honey

1 medium green pepper, cut
 into 1-inch chunks
1 medium red pepper, cut
 into 1-inch chunks
4 boneless pork loin chops
 (4 to 6 oz. each), cut into
 thin strips

4 servings

In 2-quart casserole, blend cornstarch, fennel seed, salt, orange juice and honey. Stir in green and red peppers and pork. Cover. Microwave at 70% (Medium High) for 10 to 14 minutes, or until meat is no longer pink and peppers are tender, stirring twice.

Serving suggestion: Serve with hot cooked brown rice or couscous.

Per Serving: Calories: 360 • Protein: 37 g. • Carbohydrate: 11 g. • Fat: 19 g.
• Cholesterol: 121 mg. • Sodium: 230 mg.
Exchanges: 5 lean meat, ½ vegetable, ½ fruit, 1 fat

Start with Boneless Pork

All pork is leaner today; the tenderloin is actually leaner than most meats. While boneless pork costs more per pound than bone-in cuts, there is no waste. From Sunday roast to supper stew, this adaptable meat combines with any seasoning or occasion.

◄ Cran-Raspberry Pork Medallions

2 tablespoons margarine or butter
⅔ cup chopped walnuts, divided
½ cup cranberry-raspberry sauce
2 tablespoons dry sherry
¼ cup all-purpose flour
¼ teaspoon salt
¼ teaspoon ground cinnamon
1 egg
¾ to 1-lb. pork tenderloin, sliced
    (¼-inch slices)
1 tablespoon vegetable oil

4 servings

In 2-cup measure, microwave margarine at High for 45 seconds to 1 minute, or until melted. Stir in ⅓ cup walnuts. Microwave at High for 30 seconds to 1 minute, or until bubbly. Stir in cranberry-raspberry sauce and sherry. Microwave at High for 2 to 3 minutes, or until boiling, stirring once. Cover to keep warm. Set aside.

Finely chop remaining ⅓ cup walnuts. On sheet of wax paper or microwave cooking paper, combine walnuts, flour, salt and cinnamon. In small, shallow bowl, beat egg. Dip each pork slice in egg, then in walnut mixture.

In 10-inch skillet, heat oil conventionally over medium-high heat until hot. Cook pork slices on both sides until firm and no longer pink. Spoon warm sauce over pork medallions.

Per Serving: Calories: 439 • Protein: 25 g. • Carbohydrate: 26 g. • Fat: 26 g. • Cholesterol: 116 mg. • Sodium: 275 mg. Exchanges: 3½ lean meat, 2 fruit, 3 fat

Dill-sauced Pork Loin Roast

2 tablespoons Dijon mustard
1 tablespoon honey
1 tablespoon snipped fresh dill weed
⅛ teaspoon pepper
3 to 4-lb. boneless pork loin roast

Sauce:
1 tablespoon margarine or butter
1 tablespoon all-purpose flour
1 tablespoon snipped fresh dill weed
1 teaspoon grated lemon peel
¼ teaspoon salt
1 cup half-and-half
1 tablespoon Dijon mustard

8 servings

Heat conventional oven to 325°F. In small mixing bowl, combine 2 tablespoons mustard, the honey, 1 tablespoon dill weed and the pepper. Place roast fattiest-side-up in shallow roasting pan. Spoon and spread mustard mixture on all sides of pork roast. Insert meat thermometer. Roast until internal temperature registers 165°F, about 1½ to 2 hours. Let roast stand for 10 minutes before carving.

In 4-cup measure, microwave margarine at High for 45 seconds to 1 minute, or until melted. Stir in flour, remaining 1 tablespoon dill weed, the lemon peel and salt. Blend in half-and-half. Microwave at High for 2 to 3 minutes, or until mixture thickens and bubbles, stirring once. Blend in remaining 1 tablespoon mustard. Serve meat slices with sauce.

Per Serving: Calories: 393 • Protein: 37 g. • Carbohydrate: 4 g. • Fat: 24 g. • Cholesterol: 132 mg. • Sodium: 354 mg. Exchanges: 4½ lean meat, ½ fruit, 2½ fat

Pork Tenderloin with Brandy Orange Sauce

½ cup sliced green onions
1 teaspoon grated orange peel
1 teaspoon sugar
¼ teaspoon salt
  Dash cayenne
½ cup orange juice
2 tablespoons brandy
2 pork tenderloins (¾ lb. each)
1 tablespoon plus 1 teaspoon all-purpose flour
2 tablespoons water
1 medium orange, peeled, cut in half crosswise and thinly sliced
3 cups hot cooked wild rice

6 servings

In small mixing bowl, combine onions, peel, sugar, salt, cayenne, juice and brandy. Set aside.

In 10-inch square casserole, place tenderloins side by side. Tie with string at 1½-inch intervals. Pour juice mixture over tenderloins. Cover. Microwave at 70% (Medium High) for 20 to 27 minutes, or until meat is no longer pink and internal temperature registers 165°F in several places, turning pork over once and rotating dish 2 or 3 times. Remove pork from casserole and wrap in foil to keep warm. Set aside.

In small mixing bowl, blend flour and water until smooth. Cut orange slices into quarters. Add flour mixture and orange pieces to liquid in casserole. Microwave at High for 2 to 4 minutes, or until mixture thickens and bubbles, stirring once. Slice pork and serve on wild rice. Spoon sauce over top.

Per Serving: Calories: 274 • Protein: 30 g.
• Carbohydrate: 25 g. • Fat: 5 g.
• Cholesterol: 83 mg. • Sodium: 153 mg.
Exchanges: 1 starch, 3 lean meat,
½ vegetable, ½ fruit

Szechuan Barbecue Pork & Vegetables

½ cup barbecue sauce
3 tablespoons honey
2 tablespoons soy sauce
¼ to ½ teaspoon crushed
    red pepper flakes
¾ - lb. pork tenderloin, sliced
    (½-inch slices)
1 pkg. (10 oz.) frozen whole
    baby carrots
4 oz. fresh pea pods

4 servings

In small mixing bowl, combine barbecue sauce, honey, soy sauce and red pepper flakes. Place tenderloin slices in 2-quart casserole. Add barbecue sauce mixture. Stir gently to coat. Add carrots, stirring to break apart. Cover. Microwave at 70% (Medium High) for 16 to 18 minutes, or until meat is no longer pink. Add pea pods. Re-cover. Microwave at 70% (Medium High) for 2 to 3 minutes, or until pea pods are tender-crisp and mixture is hot. Serve over hot cooked white or brown rice, if desired.

Per Serving: Calories: 229 • Protein: 22 g. • Carbohydrate: 27 g. • Fat: 4 g.
• Cholesterol: 62 mg. • Sodium: 859 mg.
Exchanges: 2½ lean meat, 2½ vegetable, 1 fruit

41

Southwestern Pork Spirals

¾ to 1-lb. pork tenderloin

Filling:

- 1 can (4 oz.) chopped green chilies, drained
- 2 tablespoons chopped red pepper
- 1 teaspoon chili powder
- ½ teaspoon ground cumin
- ¼ teaspoon garlic powder
- 3 tablespoons unseasoned dry bread crumbs

- 1 can (14½ oz.) stewed tomatoes
- 1 tablespoon olive oil
- ½ teaspoon chili powder

4 servings

Per Serving: Calories: 203 • Protein: 22 g.
• Carbohydrate: 14 g. • Fat: 7 g.
• Cholesterol: 63 mg. • Sodium: 380 mg.
Exchanges: 2½ lean meat, 3 vegetable

How to Microwave Southwestern Pork Spirals

Place pork tenderloin on cutting board. Slit tenderloin lengthwise to within ½ inch of other side. Do not cut tenderloin all the way through.

Spread tenderloin open along slit. Cover with sheet of plastic wrap. Using flat side of meat mallet, pound tenderloin to ¼-inch thickness. Remove plastic wrap. Set tenderloin aside.

Combine all filling ingredients in small mixing bowl. Spread mixture evenly over tenderloin.

Roll up tenderloin, starting with long side. Secure with string at 1½-inch intervals.

Combine remaining ingredients in 10-inch square casserole. Place stuffed tenderloin in casserole. Cover.

Microwave at 70% (Medium High) for 16 to 25 minutes, or until meat is no longer pink and internal temperature registers 165°F in several places, turning over once and rotating 2 or 3 times. Let stand, covered, for 5 minutes.

Easy Pork Fajitas

¼ teaspoon grated lime peel
¼ cup lime juice
2 tablespoons soy sauce
1 tablespoon vegetable oil
1 tablespoon packed brown sugar
¼ teaspoon garlic powder
¼ teaspoon crushed red pepper flakes
1 - lb. boneless pork loin, cut into thin strips
1 small red onion, thinly sliced (1 cup)
1 medium green pepper, sliced (1 cup)
6 flour tortillas (8-inch)
6 tablespoons sour cream
6 cherry tomatoes, quartered

6 servings

In 2-quart casserole, combine peel, juice, soy sauce, oil, sugar, garlic powder and red pepper flakes. Add pork strips. Stir to coat. Cover. Chill 1 hour.

Add onion and green pepper to marinated pork. Re-cover. Microwave at 70% (Medium High) for 9 to 12 minutes, or until meat is no longer pink, stirring once or twice.

Place tortillas between 2 dampened paper towels. Microwave at High for 1 to 1¼ minutes, or until tortillas are warm to the touch. Using slotted spoon, place about ½ cup pork mixture down center of each tortilla. Roll up. Top each with sour cream and cherry tomatoes.

Per Serving: Calories: 317 • Protein: 20 g.
• Carbohydrate: 30 g. • Fat: 13 g.
• Cholesterol: 60 mg. • Sodium: 137 mg.
Exchanges: 2 starch, 2 lean meat, 1 fat

Pork Medallions with Pears & Blue Cheese ▲

8 oz. uncooked spinach fettucini
1 tablespoon all-purpose flour
¼ teaspoon salt
Dash pepper
½ cup ready-to-serve chicken broth
2 tablespoons red wine vinegar

2 tablespoons honey
1 tablespoon Dijon mustard
¾ to 1-lb. pork tenderloin, sliced (¼-inch slices)
1 red or green Bartlett pear, thinly sliced
2 tablespoons half-and-half
¼ cup crumbled blue cheese

4 servings

Prepare fettucini as directed on package. Rinse and drain. Set aside. In 2-quart casserole, combine flour, salt and pepper. Blend in broth, vinegar, honey and mustard. Stir in pork slices. Cover. Microwave at 70% (Medium High) for 9 to 11 minutes, or until meat is no longer pink, stirring once. Stir in pear slices. Re-cover. Microwave at 70% (Medium High) for 2 to 3 minutes, or until pears are tender-crisp.

With slotted spoon, remove pork and pears. Stir half-and-half into hot liquid in casserole. Arrange pork and pears over fettucini. Top with sauce. Sprinkle with blue cheese.

Per Serving: Calories: 470 • Protein: 36 g. • Carbohydrate: 60 g. • Fat: 9 g.
• Cholesterol: 92 mg. • Sodium: 460 mg.
Exchanges: 2 starch, 4 lean meat, 2 fruit

Oriental Pork Stew ▶

1-lb. boneless pork loin, cut into 1-inch pieces
1 cup thinly sliced carrots
3 tablespoons all-purpose flour
1 tablespoon packed brown sugar
¼ teaspoon garlic powder
¼ teaspoon ground ginger
1 can (14½ oz.) ready-to-serve chicken broth
½ cup water
⅓ cup teriyaki sauce
1 tablespoon lemon juice
1 pkg. (3 oz.) Oriental dry noodle soup mix (discard seasoning packet)
1 medium zucchini, cut in half lengthwise and sliced (¼-inch slices)
2 cups shredded red cabbage

4 servings

In 3-quart casserole, combine pork and carrots. Add flour, sugar, garlic powder and ginger. Toss to coat. Blend in broth, water, teriyaki sauce and juice. Cover. Microwave at High for 10 minutes, stirring once.

Stir in noodles. Re-cover. Microwave at 70% (Medium High) for 10 to 17 minutes, or until pork and noodles are tender, stirring once. Stir in zucchini and cabbage. Re-cover. Microwave at High for 8 to 10 minutes, or until vegetables are tender, stirring once.

Per Serving: Calories: 390 • Protein: 33 g. • Carbohydrate: 33 g. • Fat: 14 g. • Cholesterol: 97 mg. • Sodium: 1330 mg. Exchanges: 1 starch, 3 lean meat, 3½ vegetable, 1 fat

Caraway Pork Reubens

6 oz. boneless pork loin, sliced (⅛-inch slices)
½ teaspoon caraway seed
⅛ teaspoon salt
⅛ teaspoon pepper
1 tablespoon vegetable oil
4 teaspoons mayonnaise or salad dressing

4 slices rye or pumpernickel bread, toasted
½ cup sauerkraut, rinsed and drained
10 to 12 thin apple slices
4 slices (1 oz. each) Swiss cheese

2 servings

Sprinkle pork slices evenly with caraway, salt and pepper. In 10-inch skillet, heat oil conventionally over medium-high heat until hot. Add pork slices. Cook on both sides until meat is no longer pink. Remove from skillet.

Spread mayonnaise on 2 slices of toast. Top with meat and sauerkraut. Arrange apple slices evenly over sauerkraut. Top with cheese.

Place sandwiches on paper-towel-lined plate. Microwave at 70% (Medium High) for 2 to 3 minutes, or until cheese is melted. Top with remaining toast slices. Microwave at 70% (Medium High) for 1 to 1½ minutes, or until hot.

Per Serving: Calories: 672 • Protein: 39 g. • Carbohydrate: 41 g. • Fat: 40 g. • Cholesterol: 118 mg. • Sodium: 924 mg. Exchanges: 2 starch, 4½ lean meat, 1 vegetable, ½ fruit, 5 fat

Start with One Pound of Ham

Ham dishes can start with steaks, slices or leftovers. Fully cooked boneless ham keeps in the refrigerator for one week. It is convenient to have on hand for emergencies.

◄ Ham Slices with Sweet Potatoes & Apples

- 2 cups peeled, cubed sweet potatoes (1/2-inch cubes)
- 2 tablespoons margarine or butter
- 1/3 cup orange marmalade
- 2 tablespoons apple juice or water
- 1/4 teaspoon salt
- 1/8 teaspoon ground nutmeg
- 1 medium green apple, cored and thinly sliced
- 4 slices fully cooked ham (3 to 4 oz. each)

4 servings

In 10-inch square casserole, combine sweet potatoes and margarine. Cover. Microwave at High for 7 to 11 minutes, or until potatoes are tender, stirring once. Set aside.

In 2-cup measure or small mixing bowl, combine marmalade, juice, salt and nutmeg. Pour over potatoes. Add apple slices. Microwave at High, uncovered, for 4 to 8 minutes, or until apples are tender and sauce is thickened, stirring once. Add ham slices. Spoon sweet potato mixture over top. Microwave at High, uncovered, for 2 to 3 minutes, or until hot.

Per Serving: Calories: 337 • Protein: 19 g.
• Carbohydrate: 42 g. • Fat: 11 g.
• Cholesterol: 45 mg. • Sodium: 1236 mg.
Exchanges: 1 starch, 2 lean meat, 2 fruit, 1 fat

Ham Pepper Steak

- 1-lb. fully cooked ham steak, about 1/4 inch thick
- 1 medium green pepper, cut into 1/2-inch chunks
- 1 medium red pepper, cut into 1/2-inch chunks
- 1 medium onion, thinly sliced
- 3 tablespoons packed brown sugar
- 1 tablespoon plus 1 teaspoon cornstarch
- 1/2 teaspoon grated lemon peel
- 1/4 teaspoon salt
- 1/4 teaspoon garlic powder
- 1/4 teaspoon ground ginger
- 3 tablespoons water
- 2 tablespoons soy sauce
- 1 tablespoon lemon juice

4 servings

Place ham steak in 10-inch square casserole. Top with green and red peppers and onion. Set aside.

In small mixing bowl, combine remaining ingredients. Pour over vegetables and ham. Cover. Microwave at High for 14 to 20 minutes, or until peppers are tender and sauce is slightly thickened, rotating casserole and stirring sauce once or twice.

Per Serving: Calories: 240 • Protein: 25 g.
• Carbohydrate: 20 g. • Fat: 6 g.
• Cholesterol: 60 mg. • Sodium: 2019 mg.
Exchanges: 3 lean meat, 1 vegetable, 1 fruit

Creamy Ham Chowder

- 1 can (15 oz.) cream-style corn
- 1 cup frozen hash brown potato cubes
- 1 can (4 oz.) chopped green chilies
- 3 tablespoons all-purpose flour
- 1/2 teaspoon salt
- 1/8 teaspoon dried thyme leaves
- 2 cups milk
- 2 cups cubed fully cooked ham
- 1/4 cup sliced green onions

4 servings

In 2-quart casserole, combine corn, potatoes, chilies, flour, salt and thyme. Blend in milk. Microwave at High for 6 to 10 minutes, or until mixture thickens and bubbles, stirring twice. Stir in ham. Microwave at High for 2 to 4 minutes, or until mixture is hot. Sprinkle evenly with green onions.

Per Serving: Calories: 312 • Protein: 23 g.
• Carbohydrate: 42 g. • Fat: 7 g.
• Cholesterol: 46 mg. • Sodium: 1816 mg.
Exchanges: 2½ starch, 2 lean meat, 1 vegetable

How to Microwave Cheesy Ham & Asparagus Lasagna

Prepare lasagna noodles as directed on package. Rinse. Let stand in cool water. Place asparagus in 1-quart casserole. Cover. Microwave at High for 5 to 7 minutes, or until tender. Drain. Set aside. In medium mixing bowl, combine ricotta, egg, parsley and onion powder. Set aside.

Microwave margarine in 4-cup measure at High for 45 seconds to 1 minute, or until melted. Stir in flour, mustard, salt and pepper. Blend in milk. Microwave at High for 4 to 6 minutes, or until mixture thickens and bubbles, stirring 3 times. Blend in Cheddar cheese until melted. Stir in asparagus and ham.

Place lasagna noodles on paper towels to drain. Cut noodles in half crosswise. In 8-inch square baking dish, layer 3 noodle halves, 2 cups of ham mixture, 3 noodle halves and 1/2 cup of ricotta mixture. Repeat layers once, ending with ricotta mixture. Cover with plastic wrap.

Cheesy Ham
& Asparagus Lasagna

- 6 uncooked lasagna noodles
- 1 pkg. (10 oz.) frozen asparagus cuts
- 1 cup ricotta cheese
- 1 egg
- 2 tablespoons snipped fresh parsley
- ½ teaspoon onion powder
- 2 tablespoons margarine or butter
- 3 tablespoons all-purpose flour
- ½ teaspoon dry mustard
- ¼ teaspoon salt
- ⅛ teaspoon pepper
- 1½ cups milk
- 1 cup shredded Cheddar cheese
- 1½ cups chopped fully cooked ham
- 1 medium tomato, thinly sliced

6 servings

Follow photo directions, left.

Per Serving: Calories: 368 • Protein: 25 g.
• Carbohydrate: 27 g. • Fat: 18 g.
• Cholesterol: 91 mg. • Sodium: 772 mg.
Exchanges: 1 starch, 2 lean meat,
1½ vegetable, ½ low-fat milk, 2 fat

Microwave at 70% (Medium High) for 14 to 16 minutes, or until temperature in center registers 150°F, rotating dish once. Let stand, covered, for 10 minutes. Arrange tomato slices on top of lasagna. Sprinkle with additional snipped fresh parsley, if desired.

Warm Hoppin' John Salad ▲

- 1½ cups julienne carrots (2 × ¼-inch strips)
- 2 tablespoons margarine or butter
- ¾ cup apple juice
- 2 tablespoons cider vinegar
- ¼ teaspoon hot pepper sauce

- ¼ teaspoon salt
- ¾ cup uncooked couscous
- 1 can (15.8 oz.) black-eyed peas, rinsed and drained
- 2 cups julienne fully cooked ham (2 × ¼-inch strips)
- 2 cups fresh spinach leaves

4 servings

In 2-quart casserole, combine carrots and margarine. Microwave at High for 4 to 7 minutes, or until carrots are tender, stirring once. Add juice, vinegar, hot pepper sauce and salt. Mix well. Cover. Microwave at High for 3 to 5 minutes, or until boiling. Stir in couscous. Re-cover. Let stand for 5 minutes, or until liquid is absorbed.

Stir in peas and ham. Tear 1 cup of the spinach leaves into small pieces and add to couscous mixture. Arrange remaining spinach leaves on 4 individual plates. Spoon couscous mixture evenly over spinach.

Per Serving: Calories: 410 • Protein: 26 g. • Carbohydrate: 53 g. • Fat: 10 g.
• Cholesterol: 37 mg. • Sodium: 1090 mg.
Exchanges: 3 starch, 2 lean meat, 1½ vegetable, ½ fat

Creamy Ham & Egg Stuffed Manicotti

6 uncooked manicotti shells

Filling:

1 pkg. (3 oz.) cream cheese
1½ cups chopped fully cooked ham
2 hard-cooked eggs, chopped (reserve 2 tablespoons)
¼ cup sliced green onions
2 tablespoons horseradish sauce
2 teaspoons prepared mustard

2 tablespoons margarine or butter
2 tablespoons all-purpose flour
¼ teaspoon salt
1 cup milk
¼ cup seeded chopped tomato

4 to 6 servings

Prepare manicotti shells as directed on package. Rinse and drain. Set aside.

In medium mixing bowl, microwave cream cheese at High for 30 to 45 seconds, or until softened. Add remaining filling ingredients. Mix well. Stuff filling mixture evenly into shells. Arrange stuffed shells in 8-inch square baking dish. Set aside.

In 4-cup measure, microwave margarine at High for 45 seconds to 1 minute, or until melted. Stir in flour and salt. Blend in milk. Microwave at High for 4 to 5½ minutes, or until mixture thickens and bubbles, stirring twice. Pour over stuffed shells. Sprinkle with tomato and reserved hard-cooked egg. Cover with plastic wrap. Microwave at 50% (Medium) for 6 to 8 minutes, or until hot.

Per Serving: Calories: 256 • Protein: 15 g.
• Carbohydrate: 18 g. • Fat: 14 g.
• Cholesterol: 107 mg. • Sodium: 666 mg.
Exchanges: 1 starch, 1½ lean meat,
½ vegetable, 2 fat

Curried Wild Rice Pilaf ▲

½ cup chopped red pepper
¼ cup sliced green onions
2 tablespoons margarine or butter
½ cup orange juice
2 teaspoons curry powder
1 teaspoon sugar

¼ teaspoon salt
2 cups cooked wild rice
2 cups cubed fully cooked ham (½-inch cubes)
½ cup raisins
½ cup slivered almonds

4 servings

In 2-quart casserole, combine red pepper, onions and margarine. Microwave at High for 3 to 5 minutes, or until vegetables are tender, stirring once. Add juice, curry powder, sugar and salt. Mix well. Stir in rice, ham and raisins. Cover. Microwave at High for 8 to 10 minutes, or until hot, stirring once or twice. Stir in almonds. Let stand, covered, for 5 minutes.

Per Serving: Calories: 405 • Protein: 22 g. • Carbohydrate: 43 g. • Fat: 18 g.
• Cholesterol: 37 mg. • Sodium: 1051 mg.
Exchanges: 1½ starch, 2½ lean meat, 1 vegetable, 1 fruit, 2 fat

Ham & Vegetable Sauced Potatoes

2 tablespoons margarine or
butter
2 tablespoons all-purpose
flour
½ teaspoon onion powder
½ teaspoon dried dill weed
¼ teaspoon salt
⅛ teaspoon pepper
1¼ cups milk
1 cup chopped fully cooked
ham
1 cup frozen mixed
vegetables
½ cup sour cream
4 frozen cheese-flavored
stuffed potatoes (4 to
5 oz. each)

4 servings

In 4-cup measure, microwave
margarine at High for 45 seconds to 1 minute, or until melted. Stir in flour, onion powder,

dill weed, salt and pepper.
Blend in milk. Microwave at
High for 5 to 8 minutes, or until
sauce thickens and bubbles,
stirring twice.

Stir in ham, vegetables and
sour cream. Microwave at High
for 2 to 3 minutes, or until hot.
Cover to keep warm.

Prepare potatoes as directed
on package. To serve, spoon
ham mixture over potatoes.

Per Serving: Calories: 439 • Protein: 17 g.
• Carbohydrate: 46 g. • Fat: 21 g.
• Cholesterol: 38 mg. • Sodium: 1211 mg.
Exchanges: 2 starch, ½ medium-fat meat,
2 vegetable, ½ low-fat milk, 3 fat

**Variation:
Ham & Broccoli Sauced
Potatoes:** Prepare recipe as
directed, except substitute ¼
teaspoon garlic powder for the
onion powder, ¼ teaspoon
dried thyme leaves for the dill
weed and 2 cups frozen broccoli cuts for mixed vegetables.
Spoon ham mixture over potatoes, corn muffins or biscuits.

Start with
One-Half Pound of Deli Meat

The deli section of your supermarket has more than prepared salads or sandwich fixings. Half a pound of deli meat serves as a basic ingredient for delicious, from-scratch main dishes.

◀ Marinara-sauced
Salami & Vegetable Platter

Sauce:

- 1 can (14½ oz.) whole tomatoes, drained and chopped
- 2 tablespoons olive oil
- ½ teaspoon dried marjoram leaves
- ½ teaspoon sugar
- ¼ teaspoon salt
- ¼ teaspoon garlic powder

- 1 medium eggplant (about ¾ lb.), cut into quarters lengthwise and sliced (¼-inch slices)
- 2 tablespoons olive oil
- 1 pkg. (10 oz.) frozen baby carrots
  Lettuce
- 8 oz. thinly sliced salami
  Green onions (optional)

4 servings

In 4-cup measure, combine all sauce ingredients. Microwave at High for 4 to 5 minutes, or until mixture thickens slightly, stirring once. Cover to keep warm. Set aside.

In 2-quart casserole, combine eggplant and oil. Cover. Microwave at High for 6 to 8 minutes, or until eggplant is tender, stirring once. Drain and remove from casserole. Set aside. Place carrots in same casserole. Cover. Microwave at High for 4 to 5 minutes, or until tender-crisp, stirring once. Set aside.

Arrange lettuce leaves on 12-inch serving plate. Roll up salami pieces. Top lettuce with eggplant, carrots and salami rolls. Spoon sauce over vegetables and salami. Garnish with green onions.

Per Serving: Calories: 341 • Protein: 11 g.• Carbohydrate: 18 g.
• Fat: 26 g. • Cholesterol: 37 mg. • Sodium: 855 mg.
Exchanges: 1 high-fat meat, 3½ vegetable, 3½ fat

Tortilla Rachel Melt ▲

- 2 to 4 tablespoons vegetable oil
- 3 flour tortillas (8-inch)
- 2 tablespoons Thousand Island dressing
- 8 oz. fully cooked turkey breast, thinly sliced
- 1 can (8 oz.) sauerkraut, rinsed and drained
- 1 cup shredded Cheddar cheese
- ½ cup sliced green onions
- ½ cup roasted sweet red peppers, thinly sliced

4 servings

In 10-inch skillet, heat 2 tablespoons oil conventionally over medium-high heat. Add 1 tortilla and cook for 5 to 10 seconds on each side, or until puffed and light golden brown. Drain on paper towels. Repeat with remaining tortillas, adding additional oil as necessary.

Place 1 tortilla on 10-inch plate. Spread with 1 tablespoon dressing and top with half of turkey. Arrange ½ cup sauerkraut, ¼ cup cheese and 2 tablespoons onions over turkey. Repeat layer once and place third tortilla on top.

Arrange remaining sauerkraut, cheese and onions and the red peppers over top tortilla. Microwave at 70% (Medium High) for 6 to 7 minutes, or until tortilla is hot and cheese is melted, rotating plate once or twice.

Per Serving: Calories: 388 • Protein: 27 g. • Carbohydrate: 20 g.
• Fat: 23 g. • Cholesterol: 79 mg. • Sodium: 534 mg.
Exchanges: 1 starch, 3 medium-fat meat, 1 vegetable, 1½ fat

Corned Beef & Vegetable Soup ▲

½ cup chopped onion
2 tablespoons margarine or
　　butter
2 cups coarsely chopped
　　cabbage
1 can (16 oz.) small whole
　　potatoes, drained and cut
　　in half
1 can (15¼ oz.) corn, drained
8 oz. fully cooked corned
　　beef, cubed (½-inch cubes)

1 jar (4 oz.) sliced pimiento,
　　drained
2 bay leaves
½ teaspoon dried marjoram
　　leaves
¼ teaspoon salt
¼ teaspoon pepper
1 can (14½ oz.)
　　ready-to-serve beef broth
1 cup water

6 servings

In 3-quart casserole, combine onion and margarine. Microwave at
High for 2 to 3 minutes, or until onion is tender, stirring once. Stir in
remaining ingredients. Cover. Microwave at High for 15 to 18 minutes,
or until cabbage is tender and soup is hot, stirring twice. Let stand,
covered, for 5 minutes before serving.

Per Serving: Calories: 214 • Protein: 10 g. • Carbohydrate: 18 g. • Fat: 12 g.
• Cholesterol: 37 mg. • Sodium: 1068 mg.
Exchanges: 1 starch, 1 high-fat meat, ½ vegetable, ½ fat

Sesame Beef Salad

2 tablespoons sesame seed
6 small new potatoes,
　　quartered (about ¾ lb.)
1 cup julienne carrots
　　(2 × ¼-inch strips)
2 tablespoons water
4 cups shredded Chinese
　　cabbage
8 oz. fully cooked roast beef,
　　cut into thin strips
½ cup mayonnaise
1 tablespoon soy sauce
2 teaspoons sesame oil
1 teaspoon sugar
¼ teaspoon crushed red
　　pepper flakes

4 servings

Heat conventional oven to
350°F. Place sesame seed in
even layer in 9-inch pie pan.
Bake for 8 to 10 minutes, or
until deep golden brown. Set
aside. In 2-quart casserole,
combine potatoes, carrots and
water. Cover. Microwave at
High for 6 to 9 minutes, or until
vegetables are tender. Drain
and cool slightly.

In large mixing bowl or salad
bowl, combine cabbage, beef
and vegetables. Set aside.

In small mixing bowl, combine
remaining ingredients. Add to
cabbage mixture, tossing lightly to coat. Sprinkle with toasted
sesame seed.

Per Serving: Calories: 464 • Protein: 23 g.
• Carbohydrate: 22 g. • Fat: 32 g.
• Cholesterol: 71 mg. • Sodium: 508 mg.
Exchanges: 1 starch, 2 lean meat,
1½ vegetable, 5 fat

For hash in a hurry, microwave it! Skillet hash takes longer, but it's still fast when you microwave the vegetables while browning the potatoes conventionally.

Quick Pastrami Hash ▲

3 tablespoons margarine or butter
1 cup frozen peas
3 cups frozen hash brown potato cubes
1 cup frozen corn
8 oz. fully cooked julienne pastrami
  (2 × ¼-inch strips)
¼ cup water
1 tablespoon Worcestershire sauce
1 teaspoon onion powder
¼ teaspoon salt
¼ teaspoon pepper
1 medium tomato, seeded and chopped

4 servings

In 2-quart casserole, microwave margarine at High for 1 to 1¼ minutes, or until melted. Add peas. Microwave at High for 2 to 3 minutes, or until tender, stirring once. Stir in remaining ingredients, except tomato. Mix well. Cover. Microwave at High for 7 to 10 minutes, or until potatoes are tender and mixture is hot, stirring once or twice. Stir in tomato. Re-cover. Microwave at High for 1 to 2 minutes, or until hot. Serve hash over tomato slices, if desired.

Per Serving: Calories: 479 • Protein: 17 g. • Carbohydrate: 46 g. • Fat: 27 g. • Cholesterol: 53 mg. • Sodium: 1051 mg.
Exchanges: 3 starch, 1 high-fat meat, ½ vegetable, 3½ fat

Skillet Corned Beef Hash

1 pkg. (9 oz.) frozen mixed vegetables
2 tablespoons vegetable oil
2 tablespoons margarine or butter
4 cups frozen cottage fries
½ cup chopped green pepper
8 oz. fully cooked julienne corned beef
  (2 × ¼-inch strips)
½ teaspoon garlic powder
½ teaspoon salt
¼ teaspoon pepper
1 tablespoon Worcestershire sauce

4 servings

Make slit in vegetable pouch. Place pouch slit-side-up in microwave oven. Microwave at High for 3 to 4 minutes, or until defrosted. Drain. Set aside. In 10 to 12-inch skillet, heat oil and margarine conventionally over medium-high heat until margarine is melted. Add potatoes. Fry for 9 to 12 minutes, or until evenly browned, stirring frequently. Stir in green pepper. Cook for 2 minutes, stirring constantly. Add remaining ingredients and the defrosted vegetables. Cook for 4 to 6 minutes, or until vegetables are tender, stirring frequently.

Per Serving: Calories: 398 • Protein: 15 g. • Carbohydrate: 40 g. • Fat: 21 g. • Cholesterol: 56 mg. • Sodium: 958 mg.
Exchanges: 2½ starch, 1 high-fat meat, ½ vegetable, 2½ fat

55

Start with Sausage

Today's sausage selection goes beyond break-fast sausage and hot dogs to include distinctively seasoned sausages like Polish, chorizo or Andouille, and low-fat sausages made from turkey. Do not substitute uncooked sausage in a recipe that calls for fully cooked, because it will not be done in the short cooking time.

◄ Hearty Turkey Sausage Pizza

1 pkg. (16 oz.) hot roll mix
1/4 teaspoon onion powder
1 cup hot water (120° to 130°F)
2 tablespoons vegetable oil
1 lb. bulk turkey sausage
1/2 cup chopped green pepper
1/2 cup chopped onion
1 medium tomato, seeded and chopped
2 cups shredded mozzarella cheese
2 tablespoons snipped fresh parsley

6 servings

Heat conventional oven to 425°F. Grease 13 1/2-inch deep-dish or 12-inch pizza pan. Set aside. In large mixing bowl, combine hot roll mix, yeast from foil packet and onion powder. Stir in hot water and oil until dry ingredients are moistened.

Turn dough out onto lightly floured surface. With floured hands, knead dough for 2 to 3 minutes, or until no longer sticky. Pat dough over bottom and up sides of prepared pan. Generously prick dough with fork. Bake for 10 to 15 minutes, or until firm and golden brown. Set crust aside. Reduce oven temperature to 400°F.

In 2-quart casserole, combine turkey sausage, green pepper and onion. Cover. Microwave at High for 6 to 8 minutes, or until meat is no longer pink, stirring twice. Drain. Spread turkey mixture over crust. Top with tomato and cheese. Sprinkle with parsley. Bake conventionally for 10 to 15 minutes, or until cheese melts and begins to turn light golden brown. Let stand for 5 minutes before serving.

Per Serving: Calories: 540 • Protein: 29 g. • Carbohydrate: 41 g.
• Fat: 30 g. • Cholesterol: 76 mg. • Sodium: 992 mg.
Exchanges: 2 starch, 3 lean meat, 2 vegetable, 4 fat

Cajun Sausage Stew ▲

1 cup thinly sliced carrots
1 cup chopped onions
1/2 cup sliced celery
2 tablespoons margarine or butter
2 tablespoons all-purpose flour
1/2 teaspoon sugar
1/2 teaspoon dried oregano leaves
1/4 teaspoon salt
1 tablespoon canned diced jalapeño peppers
1 can (28 oz.) whole tomatoes, undrained and cut up
1 pkg. (10 oz.) frozen cut okra
8 oz. fully cooked Andouille sausage links, cut into 1/2-inch pieces
8 oz. fully cooked smoked sausage links, cut into 1/2-inch pieces

4 servings

In 3-quart casserole, combine carrots, onions, celery and margarine. Cover. Microwave at High for 4 to 6 minutes, or until carrots are tender, stirring once. Stir in flour, sugar, oregano, salt and jalapeños. Mix well. Add tomatoes and okra. Re-cover. Microwave at High for 10 to 16 minutes, or until okra is tender, stirring once or twice. Stir in sausages. Re-cover. Microwave at High for 6 to 8 minutes, or until hot. Serve in bowls over hot cooked white rice, if desired.

Per Serving: Calories: 530 • Protein: 20 g. • Carbohydrate: 26 g.
• Fat: 40 g. • Cholesterol: 80 mg. • Sodium: 1615 mg.
Exchanges: 1 1/2 high-fat meat, 5 vegetable, 5 1/2 fat

Biscuit-crusted Chorizo Quiche

Crust:
- 1 cup all-purpose flour
- 2 teaspoons sugar
- 1 teaspoon baking powder
- 1/4 teaspoon salt
- 1/4 teaspoon onion powder
- 1/4 teaspoon paprika
- 1/8 teaspoon cayenne
- 1/4 cup shortening
- 1/3 cup milk

Filling:
- 8 oz. fully cooked chorizo sausage, thinly sliced
- 1/2 cup chopped red pepper
- 2 tablespoons all-purpose flour
- 1/3 cup milk
- 4 eggs
- 1/4 teaspoon salt
- 1/8 teaspoon cayenne
- 1/2 cup shredded Co-Jack cheese
- 2 tablespoons snipped fresh parsley

6 servings

Per Serving: Calories: 441 • Protein: 19 g. • Carbohydrate: 23 g. • Fat: 30 g. • Cholesterol: 186 mg. • Sodium: 806 mg. Exchanges: 1½ starch, 2 high-fat meat, 2½ fat

How to Make Biscuit-crusted Chorizo Quiche

Heat conventional oven to 425°F. In medium mixing bowl, combine all crust ingredients, except shortening and milk. Using pastry blender or fork, cut shortening into flour until mixture resembles coarse crumbs. Stir in 1/3 cup milk until dough leaves sides of bowl.

Place dough on lightly floured surface and knead 10 to 15 times, or until smooth. Press evenly into 9-inch pie plate. Prick generously with fork. Bake at 425°F for 8 to 12 minutes, or until firm and golden brown. Reduce oven temperature to 350°F.

Combine sausage and red pepper in 1-quart casserole. Cover. Microwave at High for 3 to 5 minutes, or until pepper is tender, stirring once. Drain. Set aside.

Combine 2 tablespoons flour and 1/3 cup milk in medium mixing bowl. Blend until smooth. Beat in eggs, 1/4 teaspoon salt and 1/8 teaspoon cayenne.

Microwave at High for 2 to 3 minutes, or until mixture is hot and begins to set around edge, stirring with whisk every 30 seconds. Stir in sausage mixture. Pour into prepared crust.

Bake conventionally for 15 to 20 minutes, or until center is set. Sprinkle with cheese and parsley. Return to oven for about 1 minute, or until cheese is melted. Let stand for 5 minutes.

Bologna with Onion Scalloped Potatoes

    4   cups thinly sliced russet potatoes
    1/2 cup sliced green onions
    1/2 cup sliced red onion
    2   tablespoons all-purpose flour
    1/2 teaspoon dry mustard
    1/4 teaspoon salt
    1/4 teaspoon pepper
    1   teaspoon Worcestershire sauce
    1 1/2 cups milk
    1-lb. fully cooked ring bologna

4 to 6 servings

In 10-inch square casserole, combine all ingredients, except bologna. Cover. Microwave at High for 10 minutes, stirring once. Slice bologna diagonally at 1 1/2-inch intervals to 1/4-inch depth. Place on potatoes, cut-side-up. Re-cover. Microwave at 70% (Medium High) for 10 to 18 minutes, or until potatoes are tender and sauce is thickened, stirring mixture twice.

Per Serving: Calories: 366 • Protein: 14 g. • Carbohydrate: 27 g. • Fat: 23 g. • Cholesterol: 46 mg. • Sodium: 907 mg.
Exchanges: 1 starch, 1 high-fat meat, 1 vegetable, 1/2 low-fat milk, 2 1/2 fat

This tangy springtime salad features fresh asparagus with a hint of lemon. An all-season version combines the Italian sausage and pasta with oranges and frozen green beans.

Springy Lemon Italian Salad ▶

8 oz. uncooked rainbow rotini
1 lb. uncooked Italian sausage links, sliced
   (1/2-inch slices)
1 lb. fresh asparagus, cut into 2-inch lengths
1 cup coarsely chopped red pepper
1/4 cup olive oil
2 tablespoons white vinegar
2 tablespoons lemon juice
2 teaspoons honey
1/2 teaspoon dried rosemary leaves, crushed
1/2 teaspoon grated lemon peel
1/4 teaspoon salt
1/4 teaspoon cayenne

4 servings

Prepare rotini as directed on package. Rinse and drain. Set aside. In 10-inch skillet, cook sausage conventionally over medium-high heat until no longer pink. Drain. Set aside. In 3-quart casserole, combine asparagus and red pepper. Cover. Microwave at High for 5 to 6 minutes, or until vegetables are tender-crisp, stirring once. Set aside. In small mixing bowl, combine remaining ingredients. Add to vegetables. Re-cover. Microwave at High for 1 to 2 minutes, or until hot. Add pasta. Stir to coat. Re-cover. Microwave at High for 1 to 2 minutes, or until hot. Stir in sausage. Serve on bed of fresh spinach leaves, if desired.

Per Serving: Calories: 761 • Protein: 26 g. • Carbohydrate: 52 g. • Fat: 50 g. • Cholesterol: 86 mg. • Sodium: 974 mg.
Exchanges: 3 starch, 2 high-fat meat, 1 1/2 vegetable, 6 1/2 fat

Zesty Orange Italian Salad

8 oz. uncooked mostaccioli
1 lb. uncooked Italian sausage links, sliced
   (1/2-inch slices)
1 pkg. (9 oz.) frozen Italian green beans
1/4 cup olive oil
1/4 cup orange juice
2 tablespoons white vinegar
1 teaspoon honey
1 teaspoon fennel seed, crushed
1/2 teaspoon grated orange peel
1/4 teaspoon salt
1/4 teaspoon cayenne
2 medium oranges, peeled and chopped

4 servings

Prepare mostaccioli as directed on package. Rinse and drain. Set aside. In 10-inch skillet, cook sausage conventionally over medium-high heat until no longer pink. Drain. Set aside.

Place green beans in 3-quart casserole. Cover. Microwave at High for 4 to 6 minutes, or until tender-crisp, stirring once to break apart. Drain. Set aside. In small bowl, combine remaining ingredients, except oranges. Add to beans. Re-cover. Microwave at High for 1 to 2 minutes, or until hot. Add pasta. Stir to coat. Re-cover. Microwave at High for 1 to 2 minutes, or until hot. Stir in sausage and oranges. Serve on bed of fresh spinach leaves, if desired.

Per Serving: Calories: 790 • Protein: 25 g. • Carbohydrate: 60 g. • Fat: 50 g. • Cholesterol: 86 mg. • Sodium: 970 mg.
Exchanges: 3 starch, 2 high-fat meat, 1 1/2 vegetable, 1/2 fruit, 6 1/2 fat

Summer Sausage Salad with Creamy Thyme Dressing

1 lb. red potatoes, cut in half and sliced
   (1/4-inch slices)
2 cups frozen broccoli cuts
1 cup julienne carrots (2 × 1/4-inch strips)
1/4 cup water

Dressing:
1/2 cup mayonnaise or salad dressing
1/3 cup half-and-half
1/2 teaspoon dried thyme leaves
1/4 teaspoon garlic powder

2 cups cubed summer sausage
   (1-inch cubes)
6 cups torn Bibb lettuce

4 to 6 servings

In 2-quart casserole, combine potatoes, broccoli, carrots and water. Cover. Microwave at High for 11 to 15 minutes, or until potatoes are tender, stirring twice. Drain. Set aside.

In small mixing bowl, combine all dressing ingredients, stirring with whisk until blended. In large mixing bowl or salad bowl, combine potato mixture, dressing and sausage. Toss to coat. Add lettuce. Toss gently to coat. Serve immediately.

Per Serving: Calories: 403 • Protein: 12 g. • Carbohydrate: 20 g. • Fat: 31 g. • Cholesterol: 53 mg. • Sodium: 754 mg.
Exchanges: 1 starch, 1 high-fat meat, 1 vegetable, 4 1/2 fat

Sausage & Bean Cassoulet is a thick stew, substantial enough to serve over rice. French Onion Cassoulet has the consistency of a hearty soup.

Sausage & Bean Cassoulet ▲

- 1 can (16 oz.) Great Northern beans, rinsed and drained
- 1 can (15½ oz.) kidney beans, rinsed and drained
- 1 can (15 oz.) tomato sauce
- ½ lb. fully cooked Polish sausage links, sliced (¼-inch slices)
- ½ cup julienne carrot (2 × ¼-inch strips)
- 2 tablespoons snipped fresh parsley
- 1 tablespoon packed brown sugar
- 2 teaspoons chili powder
- ¼ teaspoon ground cinnamon
- 3 cups hot cooked long-grain white rice

6 servings

In 2-quart casserole, combine all ingredients, except rice. Cover. Microwave at High for 11 to 15 minutes, or until mixture is hot and carrots are tender, stirring 2 or 3 times. Let stand, covered, for 5 minutes. Serve over rice.

Per Serving: Calories: 403 • Protein: 17 g. • Carbohydrate: 58 g. • Fat: 12 g. • Cholesterol: 26 mg. • Sodium: 777 mg.
Exchanges: 3 starch, 1 high-fat meat, 2½ vegetable, ½ fat

French Onion Cassoulet Soup

- 1 can (16 oz.) Great Northern beans, rinsed and drained
- 1 can (15½ oz.) kidney beans, rinsed and drained
- 1 can (15 oz.) tomato sauce
- 1 can (10½ oz.) condensed French onion soup
- 1⅓ cups water
- ½ lb. fully cooked Polish sausage links, sliced (¼-inch slices)
- ½ cup frozen mixed vegetables
- 2 tablespoons snipped fresh parsley

4 servings

In 3-quart casserole, combine all ingredients. Cover. Microwave at High for 15 to 19 minutes, or until soup is hot, stirring 3 times.

Per Serving: Calories: 427 • Protein: 24 g. • Carbohydrate: 45 g. • Fat: 18 g. • Cholesterol: 40 mg. • Sodium: 1792 mg.
Exchanges: 2½ starch, 2 high-fat meat, 1½ vegetable

Tortilla Coneys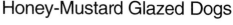

4 flour tortillas (10-inch)
4 fully cooked wieners, split in half lengthwise
1 cup shredded Cheddar cheese
1 can (15 oz.) chili beans in caliente-style sauce, divided
½ cup seeded chopped tomato
¼ cup chopped green pepper
¼ cup chopped onion

4 servings

Fold 1 flour tortilla in half. Place 2 wiener halves in center of folded tortilla. Sprinkle with ¼ cup cheese and 2 tablespoons beans. Roll up, enclosing wiener, cheese and beans. Secure with wooden pick. Repeat with remaining tortillas. Arrange around outer edges of 10-inch square casserole. Set aside.

In small mixing bowl, combine tomato, green pepper, and onion. Spoon remaining beans over Tortilla Coneys. Sprinkle evenly with vegetable mixture. Cover with wax paper or microwave cooking paper. Microwave at High for 6 to 7 minutes, or until coneys are hot and cheese is melted, rotating dish once.

Per Serving: Calories: 473 • Protein: 20 g.
• Carbohydrate: 45 g. • Fat: 25 g.
• Cholesterol: 52 mg. • Sodium: 1208 mg.
Exchanges: 2½ starch, 1½ high-fat meat, 1½ vegetable, 2 fat

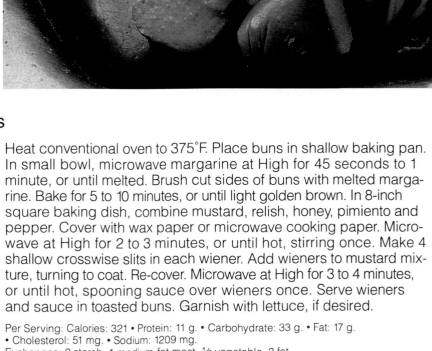

Honey-Mustard Glazed Dogs

4 pumpernickel or whole wheat coney buns, split
2 tablespoons margarine or butter
¼ cup prepared mustard
¼ cup pickle relish
1 tablespoon honey
1 tablespoon diced pimiento
⅛ teaspoon white pepper
4 fully cooked turkey wieners

4 servings

Heat conventional oven to 375°F. Place buns in shallow baking pan. In small bowl, microwave margarine at High for 45 seconds to 1 minute, or until melted. Brush cut sides of buns with melted margarine. Bake for 5 to 10 minutes, or until light golden brown. In 8-inch square baking dish, combine mustard, relish, honey, pimiento and pepper. Cover with wax paper or microwave cooking paper. Microwave at High for 2 to 3 minutes, or until hot, stirring once. Make 4 shallow crosswise slits in each wiener. Add wieners to mustard mixture, turning to coat. Re-cover. Microwave at High for 3 to 4 minutes, or until hot, spooning sauce over wieners once. Serve wieners and sauce in toasted buns. Garnish with lettuce, if desired.

Per Serving: Calories: 321 • Protein: 11 g. • Carbohydrate: 33 g. • Fat: 17 g.
• Cholesterol: 51 mg. • Sodium: 1209 mg.
Exchanges: 2 starch, 1 medium-fat meat, ½ vegetable, 2 fat

Poultry

Summer Spinach Turkey Salad

Start with One Chicken

Since most of the fat is in, or just under, the skin, remove skin from chicken pieces. Microwaved chicken stays juicy. When skinned chicken is browned conventionally, flour or crumb coatings seal in juices. Whole roasted chickens need skin and fat to prevent dryness.

Golden Italian Chicken

⅓ cup unseasoned dry bread crumbs

½ teaspoon Italian seasoning

¼ teaspoon salt

¼ teaspoon garlic powder

3 - lb. whole broiler-fryer chicken, cut into 8 pieces, skin removed

2 tablespoons vegetable oil

How to Make Golden Italian Chicken

Combine bread crumbs and seasonings in large plastic food-storage bag. Add chicken pieces to bag, one at a time. Shake to coat.

Heat oil conventionally in 10-inch skillet over medium-high heat until hot. Add chicken pieces. Cook just until brown on both sides. Continue with recipes, right.

◄ Italian Chicken with Noodles

1 recipe Golden Italian Chicken (left)

8 oz. uncooked medium egg noodles (4 cups)

2 tablespoons margarine or butter

¼ cup sliced green onions

1 medium zucchini, sliced (1 cup)

1 medium tomato, seeded and chopped (1 cup)

½ teaspoon sugar

½ teaspoon Italian seasoning

¼ teaspoon salt

¼ teaspoon garlic powder

½ cup shredded mozzarella cheese

4 servings

Prepare chicken as directed. Set aside. Prepare noodles as directed on package. Rinse and drain. Set aside. In 10-inch square casserole, combine margarine and onions. Microwave at High for 2 to 3 minutes, or until onions are tender, stirring once.

Stir in remaining ingredients, except cheese. Add noodles. Mix well. Arrange chicken over noodle mixture with thickest portions toward outside. Cover. Microwave at High for 16 to 24 minutes, or until meat near bone is no longer pink and juices run clear, turning pieces over and rearranging twice. Sprinkle with cheese. Cover. Let stand for 5 minutes, or until cheese is melted.

Per Serving: Calories: 650 • Protein: 46 g. • Carbohydrate: 55 g. • Fat: 26 g. • Cholesterol: 165 mg. • Sodium: 580 mg. Exchanges: 3 starch, 4½ lean meat, 2 vegetable, 2½ fat

Italian Chicken with Rice

1 recipe Golden Italian Chicken (left)

2 tablespoons margarine or butter

¼ cup sliced green onions

1½ cups hot water

½ teaspoon Italian seasoning

¼ teaspoon salt

¼ teaspoon garlic powder

1½ cups uncooked instant rice

2 cups frozen broccoli cuts

1 medium tomato, seeded and chopped (1 cup)

½ cup shredded Cheddar cheese

4 servings

Prepare chicken as directed. Set aside. In 10-inch square casserole, combine margarine and onions. Microwave at High for 2 to 3 minutes, or until onions are tender, stirring once. Stir in water, Italian seasoning, salt and garlic powder. Cover. Microwave at High for 4 to 6 minutes, or until water boils. Stir in rice. Let stand for 5 minutes.

Stir in broccoli and tomato. Arrange chicken over rice mixture with thickest portions toward outside. Cover. Microwave at High for 16 to 24 minutes, or until meat near bone is no longer pink and juices run clear, turning pieces over and rearranging twice. Sprinkle with cheese. Cover. Let stand for 5 minutes, or until cheese is melted.

Per Serving: Calories: 570 • Protein: 41 g. • Carbohydrate: 41 g. • Fat: 26 g. • Cholesterol: 115 mg. • Sodium: 600 mg. Exchanges: 2 starch, 4 lean meat, 2 vegetable, 3 fat

Southern-style Succotash Supper ▲

4 slices bacon, cut into ½-inch pieces	½ cup chopped red pepper
⅓ cup all-purpose flour	½ cup chopped green pepper
½ teaspoon dried thyme leaves, divided	¼ cup sliced green onions
	2 tablespoons margarine or butter
½ teaspoon salt, divided	1 pkg. (10 oz.) frozen lima beans
3 - lb. whole broiler-fryer chicken, cut into 8 pieces, skin removed	1 cup frozen corn
	¼ teaspoon cayenne

4 servings

In 10-inch skillet, cook bacon pieces conventionally over medium-high heat until brown and crisp. Drain on paper towel. Remove skillet from heat. Reserve bacon drippings in skillet. Set aside.

In large plastic food-storage bag, combine flour, ¼ teaspoon thyme and ¼ teaspoon salt. Add chicken pieces to bag, one at a time. Shake to coat. Heat bacon drippings conventionally over medium heat. Add chicken pieces. Cook just until brown on both sides. In 10-inch square casserole, combine red and green peppers, onions and margarine. Microwave at High for 3 to 5 minutes, or until vegetables are tender, stirring once. Stir in beans, corn, cayenne, remaining ¼ teaspoon thyme and salt and the bacon pieces.

Arrange chicken over vegetable mixture with thickest portions toward outside. Cover. Microwave at High for 16 to 24 minutes, or until meat near bone is no longer pink and juices run clear, turning pieces over and rearranging twice.

Per Serving: Calories: 530 • Protein: 42 g. • Carbohydrate: 37 g. • Fat: 25 g.
• Cholesterol: 110 mg. • Sodium: 570 mg.
Exchanges: 2 starch, 4½ lean meat, 1½ vegetable, 2 fat

Jalapeño Chicken Cacciatore

1 can (14½ oz.) diced tomatoes, undrained
1 can (6 oz.) tomato paste
2 tablespoons canned or fresh chopped jalapeño peppers
1 teaspoon sugar
½ teaspoon dried oregano leaves
¼ teaspoon salt
3 - lb. whole broiler-fryer chicken, cut into 8 pieces, skin removed
½ cup pimiento-stuffed green olives
8 oz. hot cooked spaghetti

4 servings

In 10-inch square casserole, combine tomatoes, tomato paste, jalapeño peppers, sugar, oregano and salt. Arrange chicken over tomato mixture with thickest portions toward outside, spooning mixture over chicken. Cover.

Microwave at High for 20 to 27 minutes, or until meat near bone is no longer pink and juices run clear, turning pieces over and rearranging twice, and spooning tomato mixture over chicken once. Sprinkle with olives. Serve over spaghetti.

Per Serving: Calories: 490 • Protein: 41 g.
• Carbohydrate: 54 g. • Fat: 12 g.
• Cholesterol: 98 mg. • Sodium: 1240 mg.
Exchanges: 2½ starch, 4 lean meat, 3 vegetable

Orange Chicken Amandine

1/3 cup all-purpose flour
1/2 teaspoon paprika
1/2 teaspoon salt, divided
1/4 teaspoon ground allspice, divided
2 bone-in whole chicken breasts (8 to 10 oz. each), split in half, skin removed
2 tablespoons vegetable oil
2 tablespoons margarine or butter
1/2 cup sliced almonds
1 tablespoon packed brown sugar
2 teaspoons cornstarch
1/2 cup orange juice
1/2 teaspoon grated orange peel

4 servings

In large plastic food-storage bag, combine flour, paprika, 1/4 teaspoon salt and 1/8 teaspoon allspice. Add chicken pieces to bag, one at a time. Shake to coat. In 10-inch skillet, heat oil conventionally over medium-high heat until hot. Add chicken breasts. Brown on both sides. Reduce heat to low and cook for 18 to 20 minutes, or until meat near bone is no longer pink and juices run clear.

In small mixing bowl, microwave margarine at High for 45 seconds to 1 minute, or until melted. Stir in almonds. Microwave at High for 2 1/2 to 4 minutes, or until bubbly, stirring every minute. Set aside. In 4-cup measure, combine sugar, cornstarch, remaining 1/4 teaspoon salt and 1/8 teaspoon allspice. Blend in orange juice and peel. Microwave at High for 3 to 4 minutes, or until mixture is thickened and translucent, stirring once. Stir in almond mixture. Serve sauce over chicken.

Per Serving: Calories: 390 • Protein: 30 g. • Carbohydrate: 19 g. • Fat: 22 g. • Cholesterol: 70 mg. • Sodium: 400 mg.
Exchanges: 1/2 starch, 3 1/2 lean meat, 1 fruit, 2 fat

69

Apricot Sweet & Sour Chicken

8 oz. uncooked vermicelli
2 bone-in whole chicken
   breasts (8 to 10 oz. each),
   split in half, skin removed
½ teaspoon ground ginger,
   divided
¼ teaspoon cayenne, divided
¼ teaspoon salt
2 tablespoons vegetable oil
1 can (17 oz.) apricot halves
   in light syrup, drained
   (reserve juice)
3 tablespoons cornstarch
2 tablespoons packed brown
   sugar
1 can (8 oz.) pineapple tidbits
   in juice, drained (reserve
   juice)
¼ cup cider vinegar
2 tablespoons soy sauce
1 pkg. (6 oz.) frozen snow
   pea pods

4 servings

Prepare pasta as directed on package. Rinse and drain. Set aside. Sprinkle chicken with ¼ teaspoon ginger, ⅛ teaspoon cayenne and the salt. In 10-inch skillet, heat oil conventionally over medium-high heat until hot. Add chicken pieces. Cook just until brown on both sides. Set aside.

Set aside 4 apricot halves. In food processor or blender, combine remaining apricots and reserved apricot juice. Process until smooth. In 10-inch square casserole, combine cornstarch, sugar, remaining ¼ teaspoon ginger and ⅛ teaspoon cayenne, the apricot purée, reserved pineapple juice, vinegar and soy sauce. Microwave at High for 5 to 8 minutes, or until mixture is thickened and translucent, stirring twice.

Arrange chicken over apricot mixture, with thickest portions toward outside. Cover. Microwave at High for 10 minutes, rotating dish once. Cut reserved apricot halves into quarters. Add apricots, pineapple and pea pods to chicken mixture. Turn chicken breast halves over. Re-cover. Microwave at High for 4 to 6 minutes, or until meat near bone is no longer pink and juices run clear. Serve over vermicelli.

Per Serving: Calories: 580 • Protein: 36 g. • Carbohydrate: 86 g. • Fat: 11 g.
• Cholesterol: 72 mg. • Sodium: 720 mg.
Exchanges: 2 starch, 3½ lean meat, 2 vegetable, 3 fruit

Chicken with Chili-Orange Salsa

    2 flour tortillas (8-inch)
  1/4 cup vegetable oil, divided
  1/3 cup all-purpose flour
1 1/2 teaspoons chili powder, divided
  1/2 teaspoon salt, divided
    2 bone-in whole chicken breasts (8 to 10 oz.
      each), split in half, skin removed
  1/2 cup sliced green onions
    1 tablespoon olive oil
    1 medium orange, peeled and chopped
      (1 cup)
    1 medium tomato, seeded and chopped
      (1 cup)
    1 can (4 oz.) chopped green chilies
    1 teaspoon sugar
  1/4 teaspoon ground cumin
    1 tablespoon white wine vinegar

                                    4 servings

Per Serving: Calories: 430 • Protein: 30 g.• Carbohydrate: 29 g.
• Fat: 22 g. • Cholesterol: 70 mg. • Sodium: 800 mg.
Exchanges: 1 starch, 3½ lean meat, 1 vegetable, ½ fruit, 1 fat

How to Make Chicken with Chili-Orange Salsa

Cut tortillas into ½-inch strips. Cut each strip in half. In 10-inch skillet, heat 2 tablespoons vegetable oil conventionally over medium-high heat until hot.

Add tortilla strips, a few at a time. Fry 1 minute, or until puffed and brown on both sides. Add oil, if necessary. Drain on paper towels. Set aside.

Combine flour, 1 teaspoon chili powder and ¼ teaspoon salt in large plastic food-storage bag. Add chicken pieces to bag, one at a time. Shake to coat.

Heat remaining 2 tablespoons vegetable oil conventionally in 10-inch skillet over medium-high heat until hot. Add chicken pieces. Cook just until brown on both sides.

Combine onions and olive oil in 10-inch square casserole. Microwave at High for 2 to 4 minutes, or until tender, stirring once. Stir in remaining ½ tea-spoon chili powder, ¼ teaspoon salt and remaining ingredients, except tortilla strips and chicken.

Arrange chicken in salsa with thickest portions toward outside. Spoon salsa over chicken. Cover. Microwave at High for 13 to 18 minutes, or until meat near bone is no longer pink and juices run clear, turning pieces over and rearranging once. Sprinkle with tortilla strips.

Monterey Chicken ▲

1 medium leek, thinly sliced
   (1 cup)
2 tablespoons olive oil
½ cup chili sauce
2 tablespoons lime juice
¼ teaspoon hot pepper sauce
1 tablespoon all-purpose flour

1 can (15 oz.) black beans,
   rinsed and drained
1 can (11 oz.) Mexican-style
   corn, drained
2 bone-in whole chicken
   breasts (8 to 10 oz. each),
   split in half, skin removed
¼ cup snipped fresh parsley

4 servings

In 10-inch square casserole, combine leek and oil. Cover. Microwave at High for 2 to 4 minutes, or until leek is tender, stirring once. Set aside. In small mixing bowl, combine chili sauce, lime juice and hot pepper sauce. Reserve ¼ cup of the chili sauce mixture.

Add flour to remaining chili sauce mixture. Mix well. Add mixture to leek. Stir in beans and corn. Arrange chicken pieces over bean mixture with thickest portions toward outside. Spoon reserved chili sauce mixture over chicken pieces. Cover. Microwave at High for 15 to 20 minutes, or until meat near bone is no longer pink and juices run clear, stirring bean mixture once and turning pieces over and re-arranging twice. Before serving, sprinkle with parsley.

Per Serving: Calories: 390 • Protein: 35 g. • Carbohydrate: 39 g. • Fat: 11 g.
• Cholesterol: 70 mg. • Sodium: 690 mg.
Exchanges: 2 starch, 3½ lean meat, 2 vegetable

Two recipes using a timesaving roasting technique that combines the speed of the microwave with the browning capabilities of the conventional oven.

Roasted Pizza Chicken

3 - lb. whole broiler-fryer
   chicken
1 tablespoon all-purpose flour
1 can (8 oz.) pizza sauce
½ medium green pepper,
   thinly sliced
1 teaspoon sugar
½ teaspoon dried oregano
   leaves
½ teaspoon garlic salt
¼ teaspoon onion powder

4 servings

Heat conventional oven to 375°F. Secure legs of chicken together with string. Set aside.

Place flour in large oven cooking bag. Hold bag closed at top and shake to coat. Add pizza sauce, green pepper, sugar and oregano to bag. In small bowl, combine garlic salt and onion powder. Rub seasoning mixture evenly over chicken. Place chicken in bag. Place in 10-inch square casserole. Secure bag with nylon tie. Make six ½-inch slits in neck of bag below tie.

Microwave at High for 15 minutes, rotating casserole once. Bake conventionally for 20 to 30 minutes, or until legs move freely and juices run clear. Let bag stand, closed, for 5 minutes. Serve with hot cooked rice or spaghetti, if desired.

Per Serving: Calories: 280 • Protein: 33 g.
• Carbohydrate: 12 g. • Fat: 11 g.
• Cholesterol: 95 mg. • Sodium: 870 mg.
Exchanges: 4 lean meat, 2½ vegetable

Lemony Greek Chicken

3 - lb. whole broiler-fryer chicken
1 tablespoon all-purpose flour
1 can (16 oz.) small whole potatoes, rinsed and drained
2 medium carrots, cut into 2 × ½-inch lengths
1 medium zucchini, cut into 2 × ½-inch lengths
¼ cup fresh lemon juice
2 tablespoons margarine or butter
2 cloves garlic, minced
½ teaspoon dried oregano leaves
½ teaspoon lemon pepper
¼ teaspoon salt
¼ teaspoon paprika

4 servings

Heat conventional oven to 375°F. Secure legs of chicken together with string. Set aside. Place flour in large oven cooking bag. Hold bag closed at top and shake to coat. Place chicken and vegetables in bag. Place in 10-inch square casserole. Set aside.

In 2-cup measure, combine remaining ingredients. Microwave at High for 45 seconds to 1 minute, or until margarine is melted. Stir. Pour mixture over chicken. Secure bag with nylon tie. Make six ½-inch slits in neck of bag below tie. Microwave at High for 15 minutes, rotating casserole once. Bake conventionally for 20 to 30 minutes, or until legs move freely and juices run clear. Let bag stand, closed, for 5 minutes.

Per Serving: Calories: 350 • Protein: 35 g. • Carbohydrate: 20 g. • Fat: 14 g.
• Cholesterol: 97 mg. • Sodium: 570 mg.
Exchanges: 1 starch, 4 lean meat, 1 vegetable, ½ fat

Start with Two Boneless Chicken Breasts

Buying boneless chicken breasts saves time and effort. You can purchase them skinned as well, although the skin is easy to remove, and skin-on breasts cost a little less. Removing the skin removes most of the fat. With imagination, you can serve this popular meat several times a week without tiring of it.

Savory Pan-fried Chicken Strips

3 tablespoons all-purpose flour
¼ teaspoon salt
¼ teaspoon paprika
¼ teaspoon garlic powder

2 boneless whole chicken breasts
   (8 to 10 oz. each), split in half, skin
   removed, cut into ½-inch strips
1 tablespoon vegetable oil

How to Make Savory Pan-fried Chicken Strips

Combine flour, salt, paprika and garlic powder in large plastic food-storage bag.

Add chicken pieces. Shake to coat. In 10-inch skillet, heat oil conventionally over medium-high heat until hot.

Add chicken pieces. Cook just until brown on both sides.

◄ Honey Lemon Chicken & Spinach Salad

1 recipe Savory Pan-fried
   Chicken Strips (above)
½ teaspoon dried rosemary
   leaves, divided
1 teaspoon grated lemon
   peel, divided
¼ cup vegetable oil
¼ cup lemon juice
2 tablespoons honey
1 medium zucchini, thinly
   sliced
1 medium yellow summer
   squash, thinly sliced
4 cups fresh spinach leaves

4 servings

Prepare chicken strips as directed, except substitute ¼ teaspoon rosemary for paprika and ½ teaspoon lemon peel for garlic powder. Set aside.

In medium mixing bowl, combine oil, lemon juice, honey and remaining ¼ teaspoon rosemary and ½ teaspoon lemon peel. Add zucchini and yellow squash. Cover. Microwave at High for 3 to 6 minutes, or until squash just begins to soften, stirring once or twice. In large mixing bowl or salad bowl, combine spinach and chicken. Add squash mixture. Toss gently to coat.

Per Serving: Calories: 411 • Protein: 35 g. • Carbohydrate: 23 g. • Fat: 21 g.
• Cholesterol: 83 mg. • Sodium: 256 mg.
Exchanges: 1 starch, 4 lean meat, 1½ vegetable, 2 fat

Parmesan Chicken Risotto ▲

1 recipe Savory Pan-fried
   Chicken Strips (page 75)
1 cup uncooked arborio rice
1 small red onion, sliced and
   separated into rings (1 cup)
½ cup chopped green pepper
¼ cup margarine or butter
1 can (14½ oz.) ready-to-
   serve chicken broth

¼ cup hot water
¼ cup white wine
½ teaspoon sugar
½ teaspoon dried basil leaves
¼ teaspoon salt
¼ teaspoon garlic powder
¼ cup grated Parmesan
   cheese

4 servings

Prepare chicken strips as directed. Set aside. In 3-quart casserole,
combine rice, onion, green pepper and margarine. Microwave at
High for 10 to 12 minutes, or until vegetables are tender, stirring
twice. Stir in remaining ingredients, except cheese. Microwave at
High, uncovered, for 15 to 18 minutes, or until rice is creamy and
most of liquid is absorbed, stirring twice. Stir in chicken. Microwave at
High for 1 to 2 minutes, or until hot. Stir in cheese. Cover. Let stand
for 5 minutes.

Per Serving: Calories: 472 • Protein: 38 g.• Carbohydrate: 28 g. • Fat: 21 g.
• Cholesterol: 88 mg. • Sodium: 920 mg.
Exchanges: 1½ starch, 4 lean meat, 1½ vegetable, 2 fat

Chicken Broccoli Stroganoff

1 recipe Savory Pan-fried
   Chicken Strips (page 75)
2 cups fresh broccoli
   flowerets
1 cup julienne carrots
   (2 × ¼-inch strips)
½ cup chopped onion
1 can (14½ oz.) ready-to-
   serve chicken broth,
   divided
3 tablespoons all-purpose
   flour
¼ teaspoon dried marjoram
   leaves
⅛ teaspoon white pepper
½ cup sour cream

4 servings

Prepare chicken strips as directed. Set aside. In 3-quart
casserole, combine broccoli,
carrots, onion and ½ cup broth.
Cover. Microwave at High for 6
to 8 minutes, or until vegetables
are tender, stirring once or
twice. Set aside.

In small mixing bowl, combine
flour, marjoram and pepper.
Blend in remaining broth. Add
broth mixture and chicken to
vegetables. Re-cover. Microwave
at High for 6 to 10 minutes, or
until sauce thickens and bubbles,
stirring twice. Stir in sour cream
until well blended. Serve stroganoff over hot cooked noodles or
rice, if desired.

Per Serving: Calories: 349 • Protein: 36 g.
• Carbohydrate: 18 g. • Fat: 14 g.
• Cholesterol: 96 mg. • Sodium: 572 mg.
Exchanges: ½ starch, 4 lean meat,
2 vegetable, ½ fat

Creamy Cucumber Dill Soup ▲

1 cup peeled seeded finely chopped
    cucumber
¼ cup chopped onion
2 tablespoons margarine or butter
½ teaspoon dried dill weed
¼ teaspoon salt
2 boneless whole chicken breasts (8 to
    10 oz. each), split in half, skin removed,
    cut into ½-inch pieces
½ cup all-purpose flour
2 cups half-and-half
1 cup ready-to-serve chicken broth

4 to 6 servings

In 2-quart casserole, combine cucumber, onion,
margarine, dill and salt. Cover. Microwave at High
for 1½ to 2 minutes, or until margarine is melted.
Add chicken pieces. Mix well. Cover. Microwave
at High for 4 to 6 minutes, or until meat is no longer
pink, stirring once. Stir in flour. Blend in half-and-
half and broth. Microwave at High for 11 to 13 minutes, or until mixture thickens and just begins to
bubble, stirring after first 5 minutes and then every
3 minutes. Do not boil. Serve garnished with
cucumber slices and sprig of fresh dill, if desired.

Per Serving: Calories: 290 • Protein: 25 g. • Carbohydrate: 13 g.
• Fat: 16 g.• Cholesterol: 85 mg.• Sodium: 345 mg.
Exchanges: ½ starch, 3 lean meat, 1 vegetable, 1½ fat

Chicken Chili Stew ▲

2 boneless whole chicken breasts (8 to 10 oz.
    each), split in half, skin removed, cut into
    ½-inch pieces
1 cup thinly sliced carrots
½ cup chopped onion
½ cup chopped green pepper
1 can (14½ oz.) diced tomatoes, undrained
1 can (6 oz.) tomato paste
2 tablespoons all-purpose flour
1 to 2 teaspoons chili powder
½ teaspoon sugar
½ teaspoon salt
¼ teaspoon cayenne
1 cup water
1 can (15½ oz.) dark red kidney beans,
    rinsed and drained

4 servings

In 3-quart casserole, combine all ingredients,
except beans. Cover. Microwave at High for 20
to 25 minutes, or until vegetables are tender and
meat is no longer pink, stirring every 5 minutes.
Stir in beans. Re-cover. Microwave at High for 2
to 4 minutes, or until hot.

*Serving suggestion: Serve stew topped with
shredded Co-Jack cheese.*

Per Serving: Calories: 347 • Protein: 40 g. • Carbohydrate: 38 g.
• Fat: 5 g. • Cholesterol: 83 mg. • Sodium: 868 mg.
Exchanges: 1 starch, 4 lean meat, 4 vegetable

How to Make Biscuit-topped Chicken Pies

Heat conventional oven to 400°F. In 2-quart casserole, combine chicken, ¼ teaspoon salt and ¼ teaspoon sage. Cover. Microwave at High for 4 to 6 minutes, or until chicken is no longer pink, stirring once. Drain. Set aside.

Place 3 tablespoons margarine in 8-cup measure. Microwave at High for 1 to 1¼ minutes, or until melted. Stir in flour, pepper, remaining ¼ teaspoon salt and ⅛ teaspoon sage.

Blend in milk. Microwave at High for 5 to 6 minutes, or until mixture thickens and bubbles, stirring twice. Stir in vegetables, pimiento and chicken.

Biscuit-topped Chicken Pies

2 boneless whole chicken breasts (8 to 10 oz. each), split in half, skin removed, cut into 1-inch pieces
½ teaspoon salt, divided
½ teaspoon dried sage leaves, divided
5 tablespoons margarine or butter, divided
3 tablespoons all-purpose flour
¼ teaspoon pepper
1¼ cups milk
1 cup frozen mixed vegetables
1 jar (2 oz.) sliced pimiento, drained
¼ teaspoon paprika
1 pkg. (10 oz.) refrigerated buttermilk biscuits

4 servings

Follow photo directions, left.

Per Serving: Calories: 570 • Protein: 40 g.
• Carbohydrate: 47 g. • Fat: 24 g.
• Cholesterol: 89 mg • Sodium: 1176 mg
Exchanges: 3 starch, 4 lean meat,
½ vegetable, 2½ fat

Tetrazzini Tart

Nonstick vegetable cooking spray
8 oz. uncooked spaghetti
2 boneless whole chicken breasts (8 to 10 oz. each), split in half, skin removed, cut into ½-inch pieces
2¼ cups half-and-half, divided
2 cups shredded mozzarella cheese
1 carton (15 oz.) ricotta cheese
½ cup chopped roasted sweet red peppers
2 eggs, beaten
¼ cup snipped fresh parsley
½ teaspoon salt
¼ teaspoon ground nutmeg
¼ teaspoon white pepper

6 servings

Spray 8-inch springform pan with cooking spray. Set aside. Heat conventional oven to 350°F. Prepare spaghetti as directed on package. Rinse and drain. Set aside. Place chicken breasts in 2-quart casserole. Cover. Microwave at High for 5 to 6 minutes, or until meat is no longer pink, stirring once. Drain. Set aside.

In large mixing bowl, combine remaining ingredients. Add spaghetti and chicken. Mix well. Spoon mixture into prepared pan. Press into pan, using back of spoon. Cover with foil. Bake conventionally for 50 minutes to 1 hour, or until firm to the touch. Loosen edges of tart with knife. Remove sides of pan. To serve, cut tart into wedges.

Per Serving: Calories: 480 • Protein: 46 g. • Carbohydrate: 33 g. • Fat: 17 g.
• Cholesterol: 170 mg. • Sodium: 540 mg.
Exchanges: 2 starch, 5½ lean meat, ½ vegetable

Microwave mixture at High for 4 to 5 minutes, or until hot, stirring once or twice. Spoon evenly into four 1-cup foil tart pans.

Place tart pans on baking sheet. In small mixing bowl, microwave remaining 2 tablespoons margarine at High for 45 seconds to 1 minute, or until melted. Stir in paprika and remaining ⅛ teaspoon sage.

Cut each biscuit in half. Dip tops in margarine mixture. Place 5 biscuit halves, coated-sides-up, on top of mixture in each pan. Bake for 9 to 12 minutes, or until golden brown.

Pecan Chicken with Cinnamon Pear Sauce

Coating:

½ cup unseasoned dry bread crumbs

¼ cup chopped pecans

½ teaspoon ground cinnamon

¼ teaspoon salt

1 egg, beaten

2 boneless whole chicken breasts (8 to 10 oz. each), split in half, skin removed

3 tablespoons vegetable oil

Sauce:

2 tablespoons packed brown sugar

1 tablespoon cornstarch

½ teaspoon ground cinnamon

1 can (16 oz.) sliced pears in light syrup, drained (reserve ¾ cup juice)

1 tablespoon brandy

4 servings

In food processor or blender, combine all coating ingredients. Process until fine. Place on sheet of wax paper or microwave cooking paper. Place egg in shallow dish. Dip each breast half, first in egg and then in crumb mixture, turning to coat both sides.

In 10-inch skillet, heat oil conventionally over medium heat. Add chicken. Cook just until brown on both sides. Reduce heat to low. Cover. Cook about 20 minutes, or until meat is no longer pink and juices run clear, turning breast halves over occasionally. Remove from heat. Cover to keep warm.

In 4-cup measure, combine sugar, cornstarch and cinnamon. Blend in reserved juice and the brandy. Microwave at High for 3 to 4 minutes, or until mixture is thickened and translucent, stirring every 2 minutes. Stir in pear slices. Spoon sauce over breast halves. Garnish with pecan halves, if desired.

Per Serving: Calories: 468 • Protein: 34 g. • Carbohydrate: 35 g. • Fat: 20 g. • Cholesterol: 137 mg. • Sodium: 321 mg.
Exchanges: 1 starch, 4 lean meat, 1½ fruit, 1½ fat

Philly Chicken Sandwiches

2 boneless whole chicken
    breasts (8 to 10 oz. each),
    split in half, skin removed
3 tablespoons all-purpose
    flour
1/4 teaspoon salt
1/4 teaspoon garlic powder
1/4 teaspoon dried thyme
    leaves
1/8 teaspoon cayenne
1 tablespoon vegetable oil
1 small onion, sliced (1 cup)
1 cup thinly sliced green
    pepper
1 tablespoon margarine or
    butter
4 slices sourdough bread,
    toasted
1/4 cup spreadable cream
    cheese
1 cup shredded Cheddar
    cheese

4 servings

Place chicken breast halves between 2 sheets of plastic wrap.
Using flat side of meat mallet,
pound to flatten slightly. In shallow dish, combine flour, salt, garlic powder, thyme and cayenne.
Coat both sides of chicken with
mixture. In 10-inch skillet, heat
oil conventionally over medium
heat. Cook chicken for 4 to 6 minutes, or just until brown on both
sides, meat is no longer pink and
juices run clear. Set aside.

In 2-quart casserole, combine
onion, green pepper and margarine. Cover. Microwave at High
for 4 to 6 minutes, or just until
vegetables are tender, stirring
once. Drain. Spread each toast
slice with 1 tablespoon cream
cheese. Place toast slices on
plate. Top evenly with chicken,
vegetables and cheese. Microwave at 70% (Medium High) for
2 to 4 minutes, or until cheese
is melted, rotating plate once.

Per Serving: Calories: 510 • Protein: 43 g.
• Carbohydrate: 28 g. • Fat: 25 g.
• Cholesterol: 130 mg. • Sodium: 660 mg.
Exchanges: 1 starch, 5 lean meat,
2½ vegetable, 2 fat

Kung Po Chicken ▲

1 cup sliced green onions,
    divided
1/2 cup chopped red pepper
1 tablespoon vegetable oil
1 teaspoon cornstarch
1/4 teaspoon crushed red
    pepper flakes
2 tablespoons hoisin sauce

2 tablespoons creamy
    peanut butter
1 tablespoon soy sauce
1/3 cup hot water
2 boneless whole chicken
    breasts (8 to 10 oz. each),
    split in half, skin removed
1/2 cup dry-roasted peanuts

4 servings

In 2-quart casserole, combine 1/2 cup onions, the red pepper
and oil. Microwave at High for 2 to 3 minutes, or until vegetables
are tender, stirring once. Set aside. In small mixing bowl, combine cornstarch, red pepper flakes, hoisin sauce, peanut butter
and soy sauce. Stir until smooth. Blend in water. Add to vegetable mixture. Add chicken breast halves. Spoon sauce over breasts.
Cover. Microwave at High for 10 to 12 minutes, or until meat is no
longer pink and juices run clear, stirring sauce and rearranging
chicken twice. Stir in peanuts. Let stand, covered, for 5 minutes.
Sprinkle with remaining 1/2 cup onions.

Per Serving: Calories: 368 • Protein: 38 g. • Carbohydrate: 10 g. • Fat: 20 g.
• Cholesterol: 83 mg. • Sodium: 584 mg.
Exchanges: 1 high-fat meat, 4 lean meat, 2 vegetable

Green Chili Chicken Enchiladas

2 boneless whole chicken
   breasts (8 to 10 oz. each),
   split in half, skin removed
½ cup thinly sliced red or
   yellow onion
1 can (4 oz.) chopped green
   chilies
1 teaspoon dried oregano
   leaves, divided
½ teaspoon ground cumin

¼ teaspoon garlic powder
   Vegetable oil
8 corn tortillas (6-inch)
1 cup shredded hot pepper
   cheese, divided
1 tablespoon margarine or
   butter
2 tablespoons all-purpose
   flour

¼ teaspoon salt
1 cup milk
½ cup shredded Cheddar
   cheese

4 servings

Per Serving: Calories: 595 • Protein: 47 g.
• Carbohydrate: 37 g. • Fat: 29 g.
• Cholesterol: 128 mg. • Sodium: 843 mg.
Exchanges: 1½ starch, 1 high-fat meat,
4 lean meat, 2 vegetable, ½ low-fat milk,
1 fat

How to Make Green Chili Chicken Enchiladas

Place chicken breast halves in 9-inch round cake dish. Top evenly with onion, chilies, 1/2 teaspoon oregano leaves, the cumin and garlic powder. Cover with plastic wrap.

Microwave at High for 6 1/2 to 9 minutes, or until meat is no longer pink and juices run clear, turning breasts over once. Drain liquid. Set aside to cool slightly.

Heat 1/8 inch oil conventionally in 8-inch skillet over medium-high heat.

Dip both sides of tortillas briefly in hot oil to soften. Place on paper-towel-lined plate. Set aside. Remove chicken breasts from chili and onion mixture.

Shred chicken. In small mixing bowl, combine shredded chicken, half of chili mixture and 1/2 cup hot pepper cheese.

Place heaping 1/4 cup chicken mixture down center of each tortilla. Roll up. Arrange tortillas, seam-sides-down, in 11 × 7-inch baking dish or 10-inch square casserole. Set aside.

Place margarine in 2-cup measure. Microwave at High for 45 seconds to 1 minute, or until melted. Stir in flour, remaining 1/2 teaspoon oregano and the salt. Blend in milk.

Microwave at High for 4 to 5 minutes, or until mixture thickens and bubbles, stirring every 2 minutes. Stir in remaining 1/2 cup hot pepper cheese until melted. Pour sauce over enchiladas.

Sprinkle with Cheddar cheese and remaining chili mixture. Cover with plastic wrap. Microwave at 70% (Medium High) for 6 to 8 minutes, or until hot, rotating dish once or twice. Let stand, covered, for 5 minutes.

Start with One Pound of Ground Turkey

In the microwave oven, ground turkey does not stick to the pan as it does when cooked conventionally. You can buy it plain or preseasoned. These recipes call for plain ground turkey; if you substitute preseasoned turkey, reduce or omit the seasonings called for in the recipes.

Easy Seasoned Meatballs

- 1 lb. ground turkey, crumbled
- 2 tablespoons unseasoned dry bread crumbs
- ¼ teaspoon salt
- ¼ teaspoon garlic powder

How to Microwave Easy Seasoned Meatballs

Combine all ingredients in medium mixing bowl. Shape mixture into 16 meatballs, about 1 inch in diameter.

Arrange meatballs in 10-inch square casserole. Microwave at High for 6 to 8 minutes, or until meatballs are firm and no longer pink, rearranging once. Drain.

◄ Oriental Meatball & Pasta Salad

- 8 oz. uncooked rotini
- 1 recipe Easy Seasoned Meatballs (above)
- ½ teaspoon ground ginger, divided
- ¼ teaspoon cayenne, divided
- 2 tablespoons soy sauce
- 2 tablespoons lemon juice
- 2 tablespoons vegetable oil
- 1 tablespoon sugar
- ¼ teaspoon salt
- 1 pkg. (10 oz.) frozen French-cut green beans
- 1 can (5 oz.) sliced water chestnuts, rinsed and drained
- 1 medium tomato, cut into thin wedges

6 servings

Prepare rotini as directed on package. Rinse and drain. Set aside. Prepare meatballs as directed, except add ¼ teaspoon ginger and ⅛ teaspoon cayenne to meat mixture before shaping. Set aside.

In small mixing bowl, combine soy sauce, lemon juice, oil, sugar, salt, remaining ¼ teaspoon ginger and ⅛ teaspoon cayenne. Add beans and soy sauce mixture to meatballs. Cover. Microwave at High for 5 to 7 minutes, or until beans are tender-crisp, stirring twice.

In large mixing bowl or salad bowl, combine rotini, water chestnuts and meatball mixture. Toss gently. Top with tomato wedges. Serve immediately.

Per Serving: Calories: 340 • Protein: 22 g. • Carbohydrate: 40 g. • Fat: 11 g.
• Cholesterol: 50 mg. • Sodium: 590 mg.
Exchanges: 2 starch, 2 lean meat, 2 vegetable, 1 fat

Rice & Meatball Supper ▲

1 recipe Easy Seasoned Meatballs (page 85)	1/4 teaspoon dried thyme leaves
1/2 cup finely chopped onion, divided	1/8 teaspoon pepper
11/2 cups uncooked instant brown rice	11/4 cups ready-to-serve chicken broth
2 bay leaves	2 cups frozen mixed vegetables
1/4 teaspoon salt	

4 servings

Prepare meatballs as directed, except add 1/4 cup chopped onion to meatball mixture before shaping. Remove meatballs from casserole with slotted spoon. Set aside.

In same casserole, combine brown rice, bay leaves, salt, thyme leaves, pepper, remaining 1/4 cup onion and the broth. Stir in vegetables. Cover. Microwave at High for 8 to 10 minutes, or until rice and vegetables are tender and liquid is absorbed, stirring twice. Stir in meatballs. Re-cover. Microwave at High for 4 to 6 minutes, or until hot, stirring once. Let stand, covered, for 5 minutes. Remove and discard bay leaves.

Per Serving: Calories: 370 • Protein: 30 g. • Carbohydrate: 44 g. • Fat: 9 g.
• Cholesterol: 75 mg. • Sodium: 640 mg.
Exchanges: 2 starch, 2 1/2 lean meat, 3 vegetable

Turkey Meatloaf with Fennel Vegetable Sauce

1	lb. ground turkey, crumbled
3/4	cup unseasoned dry bread crumbs
1	teaspoon fennel seed, crushed, divided
3/4	teaspoon salt, divided
1/8	teaspoon pepper
1	egg, beaten
1	can (14 1/2 oz.) diced tomatoes, undrained
1	can (6 oz.) tomato paste
1	cup thinly sliced celery
1	cup thinly sliced carrots
1/2	cup thinly sliced onion
1	teaspoon sugar

4 servings

Heat conventional oven to 350°F. In medium mixing bowl, combine turkey, bread crumbs, 1/2 teaspoon fennel seed, 1/2 teaspoon salt, the pepper and egg. Set aside. In 2-quart casserole, combine tomatoes and tomato paste. Add 1/2 cup of tomato mixture to turkey. Mix well. Set remaining tomato mixture aside.

Shape mixture into loaf. Place in 8 × 4-inch loaf dish. Microwave at High for 10 minutes, rotating dish once. Bake conventionally for 20 to 25 minutes, or until meatloaf is firm and internal temperature registers 185°F in center. Let stand for 5 minutes. Add celery, carrots, onion, sugar, remaining 1/2 teaspoon fennel seed and 1/4 teaspoon salt to tomato mixture. Cover. Microwave at High for 8 to 16 minutes, or until vegetables are tender-crisp, stirring twice. Serve sauce with meatloaf slices.

Per Serving: Calories: 290 • Protein: 33 g.
• Carbohydrate: 34 g. • Fat: 4 g.
• Cholesterol: 120 mg. • Sodium: 1150 mg.
Exchanges: 1 starch, 3 lean meat, 4 vegetable

Turkey Empanadas ▶

Filling:

- 1 lb. ground turkey, crumbled
- ¼ cup chopped onion
- 2 tablespoons canned or chopped fresh jalapeño peppers
- 1 teaspoon dried oregano leaves
- ½ teaspoon garlic powder
- 1½ cups shredded Co-Jack cheese, divided
- 1 pkg. (10 oz.) refrigerated pizza crust dough
  Vegetable oil

6 servings

Grease large baking sheet. Set aside. Heat conventional oven to 400°F. In 2-quart casserole, combine all filling ingredients. Microwave at High for 5 to 7 minutes, or until meat is no longer pink, stirring twice to break apart. Drain. Add ½ cup cheese. Mix well. Set aside.

Remove pizza crust from package. Unroll dough. Cut into 6 squares. Stretch or pull each to 6-inch square. Spoon about ½ cup filling into center of each square. Bring opposite corners together to make triangle. Pinch to seal edges. Place on prepared baking sheet.

Brush tops of empanadas lightly with oil. Bake conventionally for 15 to 20 minutes, or until golden brown. Sprinkle tops evenly with remaining 1 cup cheese. Bake for 3 to 5 minutes, or until cheese is melted. Serve with salsa, if desired.

Per Serving: Calories: 340 • Protein: 26 g.
• Carbohydrate: 23 g. • Fat: 16 g.
• Cholesterol: 80 mg. • Sodium: 480 mg.
Exchanges: 1 starch, 3 lean meat, 1½ vegetable, 1½ fat

Turkey Sausage & Cheese Casserole

- 1 pkg. (7 oz.) uncooked elbow macaroni
- 1 lb. bulk turkey sausage, crumbled
- 2 tablespoons margarine or butter
- 2 tablespoons all-purpose flour
- 1 cup milk
- 1 jar (8 oz.) pasteurized process cheese spread with jalapeño peppers
- 1 cup frozen peas
- 1 jar (2 oz.) sliced pimiento, drained

4 to 6 servings

Prepare macaroni as directed on package. Rinse and drain. Set aside. In 2-quart casserole, microwave sausage at High for 6 to 8 minutes, or until meat is no longer pink, stirring twice to break apart. Drain. Set aside.

In 4-cup measure, microwave margarine at High for 45 seconds to 1 minute, or until melted. Stir in flour. Blend in milk. Microwave at High for 3 to 5 minutes, or until mixture thickens and bubbles, stirring twice. Stir in cheese spread until melted. Add macaroni, peas, pimiento and cheese sauce to sausage. Mix well. Cover. Microwave at High for 6 to 8 minutes, or until hot, stirring once or twice.

Per Serving: Calories: 500 • Protein: 25 g. • Carbohydrate: 36 g. • Fat: 28 g.
• Cholesterol: 75 mg. • Sodium: 1030 mg.
Exchanges: 2 starch, 2½ lean meat, 1 vegetable, 4 fat

Parmesan Polenta Wedges

1 lb. ground turkey,
   crumbled
½ cup chopped onion
1 can (8 oz.) tomato sauce
1 can (6 oz.) tomato paste
½ teaspoon Italian seasoning
½ teaspoon sugar
½ teaspoon salt, divided
1 cup yellow cornmeal
¼ cup grated Parmesan
   cheese
¼ teaspoon garlic powder
⅛ teaspoon pepper
2½ cups hot water
½ cup chopped green pepper
2 tablespoons margarine
   or butter

6 servings

Heat conventional oven to 350°F. In 2-quart casserole, combine turkey and onion. Microwave at High for 5 to 7 minutes, or until meat is no longer pink, stirring twice to break apart. Drain. Stir in tomato sauce, tomato paste, Italian seasoning, sugar and ¼ teaspoon salt. Set aside.

In medium mixing bowl, combine cornmeal, Parmesan cheese, garlic powder, pepper and remaining ¼ teaspoon salt. Set aside. In 8-cup measure, combine water, green pepper and margarine. Microwave at High for 8 to 10 minutes, or until water is boiling. Slowly whisk in cornmeal mixture until well blended. Microwave at High for 4 to 5 minutes, or until mixture thickens, stirring once.

Spread half of cornmeal mixture in 9-inch round cake dish. Spread turkey mixture evenly over cornmeal mixture. Drop remaining cornmeal mixture by spoonfuls over turkey. Gently spread to cover. Bake conventionally for 18 to 22 minutes, or until bubbly around edges. Let stand for 10 minutes before cutting into wedges.

Per Serving: Calories: 280 • Protein: 20 g. • Carbohydrate: 26 g. • Fat: 11 g.
• Cholesterol: 55 mg. • Sodium: 810 mg.
Exchanges: 1 starch, 2 lean meat, 2 vegetable, 1 fat

Wild Rice & Turkey Stuffed Peppers

- 4 medium green peppers, cut in half lengthwise and seeded
- ¼ cup water
- 1 lb. ground turkey, crumbled
- 1½ cups cooked wild rice
- 1 cup frozen mixed vegetables
- 1 can (10¾ oz.) condensed cream of mushroom soup
- ½ cup sour cream
- ¼ teaspoon dried marjoram leaves
- ¼ teaspoon dried thyme leaves
- ¼ teaspoon onion powder
- ⅛ teaspoon pepper

4 servings

Heat conventional oven to 350°F. In 3-quart casserole, place green pepper halves and water. Cover. Microwave at High for 6 to 7 minutes, or until tender-crisp, rearranging once. Drain. Arrange cut-sides-up in 13 × 9-inch baking dish. Set aside.

Place turkey in 2-quart casserole. Microwave at High for 4 to 6 minutes, or until meat is no longer pink, stirring twice to break apart. Drain. Stir in rice and vegetables. Set aside.

In 4-cup measure, combine remaining ingredients. Add ½ cup soup mixture to turkey mixture. Mix well. Spoon turkey evenly into green pepper halves. Cover with foil. Bake conventionally for 40 to 45 minutes, or until lightly browned. Microwave remaining soup mixture at 70% (Medium High) for 4 to 5 minutes, or until hot, stirring twice. Serve over stuffed peppers.

Per Serving: Calories: 410 • Protein: 29 g.
• Carbohydrate: 30 g. • Fat: 21 g.
• Cholesterol: 90 mg. • Sodium: 730 mg.
Exchanges: 2 starch, 3 lean meat, 2 fat

Barbecue Salsa Burgers ▲

 1 lb. ground turkey, crumbled
 ¼ cup corn bread stuffing mix
 ½ cup plus 2 tablespoons barbecue sauce,
    divided
 1 egg, beaten
 2 tablespoons vegetable oil
 1 cup frozen corn
 ¼ cup sliced green onions
 1 tablespoon canned or chopped
    fresh jalapeño peppers

4 servings

In medium mixing bowl, combine turkey, stuffing mix, 2 tablespoons barbecue sauce and the egg. Shape mixture into 4 patties, about ½ inch thick. In 10-inch skillet, heat oil conventionally over medium heat. Add turkey patties. Cook on both sides until meat is firm and no longer pink, about 15 minutes. Set aside. In 1-quart casserole, combine corn, onions, jalapeño peppers and remaining ½ cup barbecue sauce. Microwave at High for 3 to 4 minutes, or until onions are tender-crisp, stirring once. Serve with turkey burgers.

Per Serving: Calories: 340 • Protein: 27 g. • Carbohydrate: 21 g. • Fat: 17 g. • Cholesterol: 130 mg. • Sodium: 560 mg. Exchanges: 1 starch, 3½ lean meat, ½ fruit, 1 fat

Olive Turkey Patties

 8 slices bacon
 1 egg, beaten
 ½ teaspoon Worcestershire sauce
 1 lb. ground turkey, crumbled
 ½ cup pimiento-stuffed green olives, sliced
 ½ cup shredded carrot
 2 tablespoons unseasoned dry bread crumbs
 ⅛ teaspoon pepper

4 servings

Layer 3 paper towels on plate. Arrange bacon on paper towels. Cover with another paper towel. Microwave at High for 6 to 9 minutes, or until lightly browned, but not crisp. Set aside.

In medium mixing bowl, combine egg and Worcestershire sauce. Add remaining ingredients. Mix well. Shape mixture into 4 patties, about ½ inch thick. Arrange patties on microwave roasting rack. Crisscross 2 bacon strips on each patty. Tuck ends of strips under patty. Microwave at High for 7 to 11 minutes, or until patties are firm and no longer pink, rotating rack once during cooking.

Per Serving: Calories: 290 • Protein: 29 g. • Carbohydrate: 4 g. • Fat: 18 g. • Cholesterol: 140 mg. • Sodium: 730 mg. Exchanges: 4 lean meat, 1 vegetable, 1 fat

Turkey Stuffing Patties with Cranberry-Nut Chutney

Patties:

- 1 lb. ground turkey, crumbled
- 1 cup herb-seasoned stuffing mix
- ¼ cup snipped fresh parsley
- ¼ teaspoon salt
- ⅛ teaspoon pepper
- 1 egg, beaten

- 1 cup whole-berry cranberry sauce
- 1 can (8 oz.) crushed pineapple in juice, drained
- 1 tablespoon packed brown sugar
- ¼ teaspoon salt
- ¼ teaspoon ground cinnamon
- ⅛ teaspoon ground cloves
- 1 tablespoon cider vinegar
- ½ cup chopped pecans or walnuts

4 servings

Grease shallow baking pan. Set aside. Heat conventional oven to 375°F. In medium mixing bowl, combine all patty ingredients. Shape mixture into 4 patties, about ½ inch thick. Arrange in prepared baking pan. Bake for 25 to 30 minutes, or until meat is firm and no longer pink.

In 4-cup measure, combine remaining ingredients, except pecans. Microwave at High for 4 to 5 minutes, or until mixture boils, stirring once. Stir in pecans. Serve chutney with turkey patties.

Per Serving: Calories: 540
• Protein: 30 g.
• Carbohydrate: 64 g.
• Fat: 21 g.
• Cholesterol: 130 mg.
• Sodium: 850 mg.
. Exchanges: 2 starch, 3½ lean meat, 2 fruit, 2 fat

Start with Boneless Turkey

An increasing variety of turkey cuts makes turkey available for use on the everyday menu. Choose a boneless or semiboneless breast for a family roast. Pretty stuffed tenderloins turn any meal into an occasion. If you relish the flavor of dark meat, try boneless drumstick steaks with a zesty sauce.

Sautéed Turkey Breast Slices

- 1 lb. turkey breast slices
- ¼ cup all-purpose flour
- ¼ teaspoon salt
- ⅛ teaspoon pepper
- 2 to 3 tablespoons vegetable oil

How to Make Sautéed Turkey Breast Slices

Cut each turkey breast slice into 3 pieces. In shallow dish, combine flour, salt and pepper. In 10-inch skillet, heat 2 tablespoons oil conventionally over medium-high heat.

Dip both sides of turkey pieces in flour mixture. Cook for 1 to 2 minutes on each side, or until browned and no longer pink, adding remaining 1 tablespoon oil, if necessary.

◄ Summer Spinach Turkey Salad

- 1 recipe Sautéed Turkey Breast Slices (above)
- 2 teaspoons dried parsley flakes
- ½ teaspoon ground coriander, divided
- ¼ teaspoon ground allspice, divided
- 4 slices bacon, cut into ½-inch pieces
- 2 tablespoons cider vinegar
- 2 tablespoons lemon juice
- 2 tablespoons honey
- ⅛ teaspoon salt
- 4 cups torn fresh spinach leaves
- 2 cups sliced fresh or defrosted frozen peaches
- 2 cups sliced fresh strawberries

4 servings

Prepare turkey breast slices as directed, except add parsley flakes, ¼ teaspoon coriander and ⅛ teaspoon allspice to flour mixture. Set aside. Place bacon pieces in 1-quart casserole. Cover with paper towel. Microwave at High for 4 to 6 minutes, or until brown and crisp, stirring once to break apart. Remove bacon from casserole with slotted spoon. Set aside.

To drippings, add vinegar, lemon juice, honey, salt, the remaining ¼ teaspoon coriander and ⅛ teaspoon allspice. Mix well. Microwave at High for 2 to 3 minutes, or until mixture comes to a boil, stirring once. In large mixing bowl or salad bowl, combine spinach, peaches, strawberries, turkey and bacon pieces. Add hot vinegar mixture. Toss gently. Serve immediately.

Per Serving: Calories: 360 • Protein: 31 g. • Carbohydrate: 37 g. • Fat: 11 g.
• Cholesterol: 75 mg. • Sodium: 390 mg.
Exchanges: ½ starch, 4 lean meat, 1 vegetable, 1½ fruit

Pasta Salad with Fresh Tomato Sauce

  8 oz. uncooked mini lasagna noodles
  1 recipe Sautéed Turkey Breast Slices (page 93)
1½ teaspoons dried basil leaves, divided
  ¼ teaspoon garlic powder
  4 cups fresh broccoli flowerets
  2 tablespoons water
  2 medium tomatoes, seeded and chopped (2 cups)
  2 tablespoons olive oil
  1 tablespoon white wine vinegar
  1 teaspoon sugar
  ¼ teaspoon salt
  2 tablespoons grated Parmesan cheese

6 servings

Prepare noodles as directed on package. Rinse and drain. Set aside. Prepare turkey breast slices as directed, except add ½ teaspoon basil leaves and the garlic powder to flour mixture. Set aside.

In 3-quart casserole, combine broccoli and water. Cover. Microwave at High for 3 to 5 minutes, or until broccoli is tender-crisp, stirring once. Drain. Stir in tomatoes, oil, vinegar, sugar, salt and remaining 1 teaspoon basil leaves. Mix well. Microwave at High, uncovered, for 2 to 4 minutes, or until hot, stirring once. Stir in noodles and turkey slices. Toss to coat. Sprinkle with Parmesan cheese. Serve immediately.

Per Serving: Calories: 350 • Protein: 25 g. • Carbohydrate: 37 g. • Fat: 11 g.
• Cholesterol: 50 mg. • Sodium: 270 mg.
Exchanges: 1½ starch, 2 lean meat, 2½ vegetable, 1 fat

Turkey Piccata Salad

8 oz. uncooked mostaccioli
1 recipe Sautéed Turkey
   Breast Slices (page 93)
1 teaspoon dried tarragon
   leaves, divided
1 teaspoon grated lemon
   peel, divided
8 oz. fresh mushrooms,
   quartered
1 tablespoon water
2 medium tomatoes, seeded
   and chopped (2 cups)
2 tablespoons olive oil
1 tablespoon lemon juice
1/2 teaspoon sugar
1/4 teaspoon salt

6 servings

Prepare mostaccioli as directed on package. Rinse and drain. Set aside. Prepare turkey breast slices as directed, except add 1/2 teaspoon tarragon leaves and 1/2 teaspoon lemon peel to flour mixture. Set aside.

In 3-quart casserole, combine mushrooms and water. Cover. Microwave at High for 2 to 4 minutes, or until hot, stirring once. Drain. Stir in tomatoes, oil, lemon juice, sugar, salt, remaining 1/2 teaspoon tarragon leaves and 1/2 teaspoon lemon peel. Mix well. Microwave at High for 2 to 4 minutes, or until hot, stirring once. Stir in mostaccioli and turkey. Toss to coat. Serve immediately.

Per Serving: Calories: 330 • Protein: 23 g. • Carbohydrate: 36 g. • Fat: 10 g.
• Cholesterol: 45 mg. • Sodium: 210 mg.
Exchanges: 1 1/2 starch, 2 lean meat, 2 1/2 vegetable, 1 fat

Country Turkey Breast with Vegetables

1 tablespoon all-purpose flour
2 to 3-lb. boneless or
   semiboneless turkey breast
   roast
½ teaspoon salt
½ teaspoon dried marjoram
   leaves
½ teaspoon onion powder
⅛ teaspoon pepper
2 tablespoons margarine or
   butter
1 pkg. (10 oz.) frozen
   Brussels sprouts
6 miniature ears (2½ to 3-inch)
   frozen corn on the cob

6 servings

Heat conventional oven to 350°F. Place flour in oven cooking bag. Hold bag closed at top and shake to coat. Place turkey breast fat-side-up in bag. Sprinkle with salt, marjoram leaves, onion powder and pepper. Top with margarine. Secure bag with nylon tie. Make six ½-inch slits in neck of bag below tie. Place bag in 10-inch square casserole. Microwave at High for 15 minutes.

Open bag. Arrange Brussels sprouts and corn around turkey. Close bag with nylon tie. Bake conventionally for 30 to 40 minutes, or until internal temperature registers 170°F in several places. Let bag stand, closed, for 10 minutes.

Per Serving: Calories: 250 • Protein: 37 g. • Carbohydrate: 14 g. • Fat: 5 g.
• Cholesterol: 95 mg. • Sodium: 290 mg.
Exchanges: ½ starch, 4 lean meat, 1 vegetable

96

Maui Pineapple Turkey

1 fresh pineapple (about
    3½ to 4 lbs.)
2 turkey tenderloins (10 oz.
    each), sliced (¼ inch slices)
¼ cup plus 2 tablespoons
    teriyaki sauce, divided
1 cup coarsely chopped green
    pepper
¼ cup sliced green onions
2 tablespoons cornstarch
1 tablespoon packed brown sugar
⅛ teaspoon ground ginger
¼ cup unsweetened pineapple juice
1 cup seedless red grapes
¼ cup toasted coconut

4 servings

Cut pineapple into quarters lengthwise; leave leafy
portions attached. With thin, flexible knife, loosen
and remove fruit, leaving ½-inch shells. Place shells
in 13 × 9-inch baking dish. Cover with plastic wrap.
Refrigerate. Cut off and discard core of pineapple.
Cut fruit into 1-inch chunks. Set aside.

In 2-quart casserole, combine turkey and 2 tablespoons teriyaki sauce. Cover. Microwave at High
for 4 minutes, stirring once. Stir in green pepper
and onions. Re-cover. Microwave at High for 4 to
6 minutes, or until meat is no longer pink and vegetables are tender-crisp, stirring twice. Drain and
reserve liquid from turkey mixture. Add water to

equal ¾ cup. Set turkey mixture aside. In medium
mixing bowl, combine cornstarch, sugar and
ginger. Blend in juice and remaining ¼ cup teriyaki sauce. Stir in reserved turkey liquid until well
blended. Microwave at High for 2 to 4 minutes, or
until mixture is thickened and translucent, stirring
once. Add to turkey mixture. Add pineapple and
grapes. Toss to coat. Place 1 pineapple shell on
each plate. Top with one-fourth of turkey mixture.
Sprinkle with coconut. Serve with hot cooked rice,
if desired.

Per Serving: Calories: 490 • Protein: 38 g. • Carbohydrate: 75 g.
• Fat: 4 g. • Cholesterol: 90 mg. • Sodium: 1100 mg.
Exchanges: 1 starch, 4 lean meat, 1 vegetable, 3½ fruit

97

Seasoned Turkey Medallions

2 turkey tenderloins (about 10 oz. each)
2 tablespoons water
1 teaspoon honey
Dash pepper

How to Microwave Seasoned Turkey Medallions

Cut each tenderloin diagonally into eight 1-inch slices. In 2-quart casserole, combine water, honey and pepper.

Add turkey slices. Toss to coat. Cover. Microwave at 70% (Medium High) for 10 to 14 minutes, or until meat is firm and no longer pink, stirring once. Drain and discard liquid.

Creamy Dijon Dill Turkey Salad ▲

Dressing:
½ cup mayonnaise or salad dressing
2 tablespoons Dijon mustard
2 teaspoons honey
¼ teaspoon salt
¼ teaspoon dried dill weed

Salad:
1 recipe Seasoned Turkey Medallions (right)

1 tablespoon Dijon mustard
Lettuce leaves (optional)
2 cups warm cooked brown rice
1 medium cucumber, cut in half lengthwise and sliced
1 medium tomato, seeded and coarsely chopped
1 medium avocado, peeled and sliced

6 servings

In small mixing bowl, combine all dressing ingredients. Set aside. Prepare turkey medallions as directed, except add mustard to water mixture. Set aside. Arrange lettuce leaves on large serving plate. Spoon rice over lettuce. Top with cucumber, tomato, turkey and avocado. Spoon dressing over salad.

Per Serving: Calories: 380 • Protein: 25 g. • Carbohydrate: 23 g. • Fat: 22 g.
• Cholesterol: 70 mg. • Sodium: 340 mg.
Exchanges: 1 starch, 2½ lean meat, 1½ vegetable, 2½ fat

Creamy Curry Turkey Salad

Dressing:

½ cup mayonnaise or salad
    dressing
2 teaspoons honey
1 teaspoon lemon juice
2 teaspoons curry powder
¼ teaspoon salt

Salad:

1 recipe Seasoned Turkey
    Medallions (opposite)
½ teaspoon curry powder
½ cup julienne carrot
    (1½ × ¼-inch strips)
    Lettuce leaves (optional)
2 cups warm cooked brown
    rice
1 medium apple, cored and
    cut into thin wedges
¼ cup raisins

6 servings

In small mixing bowl, combine all dressing ingredients. Set aside. Prepare turkey medallions as directed, except add ½ teaspoon curry powder and the carrot to water mixture and set turkey slices aside. Cover carrot mixture. Microwave at High for 3 to 5 minutes, or until carrots are tender-crisp, stirring once. Remove carrots with slotted spoon. Set aside.

Add turkey pieces to liquid in casserole and continue with turkey medallion recipe.

Arrange lettuce leaves on large serving plate. Spoon rice over lettuce. Top with carrot, turkey and apple. Spoon dressing over salad. Sprinkle with raisins.

Per Serving: Calories: 350 • Protein: 24 g. • Carbohydrate: 28 g. • Fat: 16 g.
• Cholesterol: 70 mg. • Sodium: 240 mg.
Exchanges: 1 starch, 2½ lean meat, 1 vegetable, ½ fruit, 2 fat

Two quick turkey and stuffing recipes, perfect for everyday or easy entertaining.

How to Cut Pocket in Turkey Tenderloin

Place turkey tenderloin on cutting board. Using thin, sharp knife, slice lengthwise down center to within ½ inch of bottom and ends (do not cut through). Cut into sides of tenderloin from center to make pocket on each side.

Cajun Corn Bread Stuffed Tenderloins

Seasoning Mix:

½ teaspoon salt
½ teaspoon dried basil leaves
½ teaspoon dried thyme leaves
½ teaspoon dried oregano leaves
¼ teaspoon pepper
¼ teaspoon cayenne

2 turkey tenderloins (about 10 oz. each)
¼ cup chopped green onions
¼ cup finely chopped carrot
¼ cup finely chopped green pepper
¼ cup plus 1 tablespoon margarine or butter, divided
1 cup corn bread stuffing mix
2 tablespoons water

4 servings

Heat conventional oven to 375°F. In small bowl, combine all seasoning mix ingredients. Set aside. Make pocket in tenderloins as directed above. Set aside.

In 2-quart casserole, combine onions, carrot, green pepper and ¼ cup margarine. Microwave at High for 3 to 4 minutes, or until vegetables are tender-crisp, stirring once. Stir in stuffing mix, water and 1 teaspoon of seasoning mix. Mix well. Fill each pocket with half of stuffing mixture. Secure with wooden picks. Place tenderloins in 8-inch square baking dish. Set aside.

In small bowl, microwave remaining 1 tablespoon margarine at High for 45 seconds to 1 minute, or until melted. Stir in remaining seasoning mix. Brush evenly over tenderloins. Cover with wax paper or microwave cooking paper. Microwave at High for 10 minutes. Remove wax paper. Bake conventionally, uncovered, for 15 to 20 minutes, or until meat is firm and no longer pink.

Per Serving: Calories: 410 • Protein: 37 g. • Carbohydrate: 28 g. • Fat: 17 g.
• Cholesterol: 90 mg. • Sodium: 960 mg.
Exchanges: 1½ starch, 4 lean meat, 1 vegetable, 1 fat

Broccoli Cheese Stuffed Tenderloins

Seasoning Mix:

    1 teaspoon Italian seasoning
  1/2 teaspoon salt
  1/2 teaspoon garlic powder
  1/4 teaspoon paprika
  1/4 teaspoon pepper

    2 turkey tenderloins (about
      10 oz. each)
1 1/2 cups frozen broccoli cuts
  1/4 cup chopped green onions
  1/4 cup plus 1 tablespoon
      margarine or butter,
      divided
  1/2 cup shredded Cheddar
      cheese
  1/3 cup unseasoned dry
      bread crumbs

4 servings

Heat conventional oven to 375°F. In small bowl, combine all seasoning mix ingredients. Set aside. Make pocket in tenderloins as directed (opposite). Set aside. In 2-quart casserole, microwave broccoli at High for 45 seconds to 1 minute, or until defrosted. Chop and return to casserole. Add onions and 1/4 cup margarine. Cover. Microwave at High for 2 to 4 minutes, or until vegetables are tender-crisp, stirring once. Stir in cheese, bread crumbs and 3/4 teaspoon of seasoning mix. Mix well. Fill each pocket with half of stuffing mixture. Secure with wooden picks. Place tenderloins in 8-inch square baking dish. Set aside.

In small bowl, microwave remaining 1 tablespoon margarine at High for 45 seconds to 1 minute, or until melted. Stir in remaining seasoning mix. Brush evenly over tenderloins. Cover with wax paper or microwave cooking paper. Microwave at High for 10 minutes. Remove wax paper. Bake conventionally, uncovered, for 15 to 20 minutes, or until meat is firm and no longer pink.

Per Serving: Calories: 370 • Protein: 38 g. • Carbohydrate: 9 g. • Fat: 20 g.
• Cholesterol: 103 mg. • Sodium: 650 mg.
Exchanges: 1/2 starch, 6 lean meat, 1/2 vegetable

Thick & Zesty Minestrone ▶

    1 lb. turkey drumstick steaks, cut into 1/2-inch
      pieces
    1 cup sliced carrots
  1/2 cup chopped onion
    1 teaspoon Italian seasoning
  1/4 teaspoon garlic powder
  1/4 teaspoon salt
  1/4 teaspoon pepper
  1/8 teaspoon cayenne
    1 can (16 oz.) whole tomatoes, undrained and
      cut up
    1 can (14 1/2 oz.) ready-to-serve beef broth
  1/2 cup water
    1 cup broken uncooked vermicelli
    1 can (15 oz.) garbanzo beans, rinsed and
      drained
    1 pkg. (9 oz.) frozen Italian green beans

6 servings

In 3-quart casserole, combine all ingredients, except vermicelli and beans. Cover. Microwave at High for 10 minutes, stirring once. Stir in vermicelli. Re-cover. Microwave at High for 10 minutes, stirring once. Stir in beans. Re-cover. Microwave at High for 10 to 13 minutes, or until vegetables are tender and meat is no longer pink, stirring once.

Per Serving: Calories: 220 • Protein: 18 g. • Carbohydrate: 31 g.
• Fat: 3 g. • Cholesterol: 40 mg. • Sodium: 470 mg.
Exchanges: 1 starch, 1 lean meat, 3 vegetable

Lightly
Coated
Shrimp

Start with One Pound of Fish Fillets

Vary fish dinners, using two basic recipes and a selection of sauces. Fast microwave fillets have delicate flavor and natural moisture. A crumb coating crisps oven-fried fillets and prevents drying. For fish fillets, choose sole, flounder, orange roughy, walleye or cod.

◄ Basic Microwave Fillets

1 lb. fish fillets, 1/4 to 1/2 inch thick, cut into serving-size pieces
1 tablespoon margarine or butter
1 tablespoon lemon juice
1/4 teaspoon onion or garlic powder
1/4 teaspoon salt
1/8 teaspoon pepper

4 servings

Arrange fillets in 8-inch square baking dish. Set aside. In small bowl, microwave margarine at High for 45 seconds to 1 minute, or until melted. Stir in lemon juice. Brush evenly over fillets. Sprinkle with onion powder, salt and pepper.

Cover with microwave cooking paper or wax paper. Microwave at High for 4 to 6 minutes, or until fish flakes easily with fork, rotating dish and rearranging fillets once.

Per Serving: Calories: 130 • Protein: 21 g.
• Carbohydrate: 1 g. • Fat: 4 g.
• Cholesterol: 55 mg. • Sodium: 260 mg.
Exchanges: 3 lean meat

Basic Oven-fried Fillets

1/2 cup cornflake crumbs
1/4 cup snipped fresh parsley
2 tablespoons yellow cornmeal
1/2 teaspoon salt
1/2 teaspoon paprika
1/8 teaspoon cayenne
1 egg
2 tablespoons lemon juice
1/4 cup margarine or butter
1 lb. fish fillets, 1/4 to 1/2 inch thick, cut into serving-size pieces

4 servings

Heat conventional oven to 400°F. In shallow dish, combine crumbs, parsley, cornmeal, salt, paprika and cayenne. Set aside. In another shallow dish, beat egg slightly. Beat in lemon juice. Set aside. In small bowl, microwave margarine at High for 1 1/4 to 1 1/2 minutes, or until melted. Spread 1 tablespoon of margarine in 13 × 9-inch baking dish.

Dip each side of fish in egg mixture, then in crumb mixture, coating well. Place in prepared dish. Drizzle remaining melted margarine over fish. Bake for 12 to 15 minutes, or until fish flakes easily with fork.

Per Serving: Calories: 270 • Protein: 23 g.
• Carbohydrate: 13 g. • Fat: 14 g.
• Cholesterol: 102 mg. • Sodium: 590 mg.
Exchanges: 1 starch, 3 lean meat, 1 fat

◄ Sweet & Sour Lemon Sauce

2 tablespoons packed brown sugar
1 tablespoon cornstarch
1/4 teaspoon garlic salt
1/2 cup ready-to-serve chicken broth
2 tablespoons lemon juice
1 tablespoon red wine vinegar
1 tablespoon catsup
1 can (8 oz.) pineapple tidbits in juice, drained
10 maraschino cherries, cut in half

4 servings, 1/2 cup each

In 4-cup measure, combine sugar, cornstarch and garlic salt. Blend in broth, lemon juice, vinegar and catsup. Mix well. Microwave at High for 3 to 5 minutes, or until mixture is thickened and translucent, stirring once or twice. Add pineapple and cherries. Mix well. Serve with Basic Microwave or Oven-fried Fillets (left).

Per Serving: Calories: 80 • Protein: 1 g.
• Carbohydrate: 21 g. • Fat: 0
• Cholesterol: 0 • Sodium: 270 mg.
Exchanges: 1 1/2 fruit

Light & Lean Tartar Sauce ▲

½ cup reduced-calorie
   mayonnaise
¼ cup lean sour cream
1 tablespoon lemon juice
1 tablespoon sweet pickle
   relish
1 tablespoon capers, drained
1 tablespoon snipped fresh
   parsley

12 servings,
1 tablespoon each

In small mixing bowl, combine
all ingredients. Cover with plastic wrap. Chill at least 4 hours, or
until flavors are blended. Serve
with Basic Microwave or Oven-
fried Fillets (page 105).

Per Serving: Calories: 35 • Protein: 0
• Carbohydrate: 2 g. • Fat: 3 g.
• Cholesterol: 5 mg. • Sodium: 75 mg.
Exchanges: ½ vegetable, ½ fat

Tropical Mango Sauce ▲

1 can (15 oz.) sliced
   mangoes in light syrup,
   drained
½ teaspoon grated lime peel
1 teaspoon fresh lime juice

12 servings,
1 tablespoon each

In food processor or blender,
combine all ingredients. Process
until smooth. Serve with Basic
Microwave or Oven-fried Fillets
(page 105).

Variation:

Tropical Peach Sauce: Follow
recipe above, except substitute
1 can (16 oz.) sliced peaches in
light syrup, drained, for mangoes.

Per Serving: Calories: 8 • Protein: 0
• Carbohydrate: 2 g. • Fat: 0
• Cholesterol: 0 • Sodium: 1 mg.
Exchanges: free

Fresh Cucumber ▲
Dill Sauce

1 cucumber (12 oz.), peeled
   and cut into 1-inch chunks
½ cup buttermilk
½ cup mayonnaise
1 tablespoon snipped fresh
   dill weed

24 servings,
1 tablespoon each

In food processor or blender,
process cucumber chunks
until smooth. Drain. Return
cucumber purée to food processor or blender. Add remaining
ingredients. Process until well
blended. In 4-cup measure,
microwave cucumber mixture
at High for 2 to 3 minutes, or
until hot, stirring once. Serve
with Basic Microwave or Oven-
fried Fillets (page 105).

Per Serving: Calories: 35 • Protein: 0
• Carbohydrate: 1 g. • Fat: 4 g.
• Cholesterol: 3 mg. • Sodium: 30 mg.
Exchanges: 1 fat

Sole with Vegetables ▶ & Spinach Noodles

8 oz. uncooked spinach egg
   noodles
¼ cup olive oil, divided
1 can (15 oz.) baby cob corn,
   rinsed and drained
½ cup sliced green onions
¼ cup margarine or butter
½ teaspoon dried tarragon
   leaves
¼ teaspoon salt
1 lb. sole fillets, ¼ to ½ inch
   thick, cut into serving-size
   pieces
1 large tomato, coarsely
   chopped

4 servings

Prepare noodles as directed on package. Rinse and drain. Toss with 2 tablespoons oil. Cover to keep warm.

In 10-inch square casserole, combine corn, onions and margarine. Cover. Microwave at High for 3 to 4 minutes, or until corn is hot, stirring once. Stir in tarragon, salt and remaining 2 tablespoons oil. Add fillets. Spoon corn mixture over fish. Re-cover. Microwave at High for 4 to 6 minutes, or until fish flakes easily with fork.

Remove fish from casserole. Stir tomato into corn mixture. Microwave at High, uncovered, for 1 to 2 minutes, or until hot. Serve fillets over noodles. Top with vegetable mixture.

Per Serving: Calories: 620 • Protein: 33 g.
• Carbohydrate: 58 g. • Fat: 30 g.
• Cholesterol: 115 mg. • Sodium: 390 mg.
Exchanges: 3 starch, 2½ lean meat,
2½ vegetable, 4½ fat

Spicy Vegetable-sauced Fillets

1 cup julienne carrots
   (2 × ⅛-inch strips)
½ cup chopped onion
1 can (14½ oz.) diced
   tomatoes, undrained
¼ cup barbecue sauce
2 tablespoons tomato paste
½ teaspoon dried oregano
   leaves
½ teaspoon salt, divided
⅛ teaspoon cayenne

1 cup julienne zucchini
   (2 × ⅛-inch strips)
½ cup sliced black olives
1 lb. sole fillets, ¼ to ½ inch
   thick, cut into serving-size
   pieces
1 tablespoon margarine or
   butter
1 tablespoon lemon juice
⅛ teaspoon pepper

4 servings

In 2-quart casserole, combine carrots, onion, tomatoes, barbecue sauce, tomato paste, oregano, ¼ teaspoon salt and the cayenne. Cover. Microwave at High for 6 to 9 minutes, or until vegetables are tender-crisp, stirring once. Stir in zucchini and olives. Re-cover. Microwave at High for 2 to 4 minutes, or until sauce is hot and zucchini is tender, stirring once. Cover to keep warm.

Arrange fillets in 8-inch square baking dish. Set aside. In small bowl, microwave margarine at High for 45 seconds to 1 minute, or until melted. Stir in lemon juice, pepper and remaining ¼ teaspoon salt. Brush evenly over fillets. Cover fillets with wax paper or microwave cooking paper. Microwave at High for 4 to 6 minutes, or until fish flakes easily with fork, rotating dish and rearranging fillets once. Spoon sauce evenly onto serving plates. Arrange fillets over sauce.

Per Serving: Calories: 210 • Protein: 24 g. • Carbohydrate: 15 g. • Fat: 7 g.
• Cholesterol: 55 mg. • Sodium: 910 mg.
Exchanges: 2½ lean meat, 3 vegetable

Lattice-topped Cod Casserole

½ cup thinly sliced carrot
½ cup thinly sliced celery
½ cup chopped onion
2 tablespoons margarine or butter
¼ cup all-purpose flour
2 teaspoons dried parsley flakes
½ teaspoon dried thyme leaves
¼ teaspoon dried rubbed sage leaves
1 can (12 oz.) evaporated milk
1 lb. cod fillets, ¼ to ½ inch thick, cut into 1-inch pieces
1 can (16 oz.) sliced potatoes, rinsed and drained
1 pkg. (11 oz.) refrigerated bread sticks

4 to 6 servings

Per Serving: Calories: 370 • Protein: 24 g.
• Carbohydrate: 42 g. • Fat: 12 g.
• Cholesterol: 51 mg. • Sodium: 595 mg.
Exchanges: 2 starch, 1½ lean meat, 1 vegetable, ½ whole milk, ½ fat

How to Make Lattice-topped Cod Casserole

Heat conventional oven to 350°F. In 8-inch square baking dish, combine carrot, celery, onion and margarine. Cover with plastic wrap. Microwave at High for 5 to 7 minutes, or until vegetables are tender, stirring once.

Stir in flour, parsley, thyme and sage. Blend in milk. Add fish pieces. Mix well. Microwave at High, uncovered, for 8 to 12 minutes, or until mixture begins to thicken and bubble around edges, stirring every 3 minutes. Add potatoes. Mix well.

Arrange 4 bread sticks, evenly spaced, across top of casserole. Weave remaining 4 bread sticks to form lattice. Trim bread sticks at edge of dish. Bake for 20 to 23 minutes, or until bread sticks are golden brown.

Salmon Steaks with Creamy Succotash

1 cup chopped red pepper
1 cup chopped green pepper
2 tablespoons margarine or butter
1½ cups frozen corn
1½ teaspoons grated lemon peel
1 teaspoon dried basil leaves
½ teaspoon onion powder
½ teaspoon salt
⅛ teaspoon pepper
4 salmon steaks (6 to 8 oz. each)
2 teaspoons all-purpose flour
½ cup half-and-half

4 servings

In 10-inch square casserole, combine red and green peppers and margarine. Cover. Microwave at High for 4 to 6 minutes, or until peppers are tender-crisp, stirring once. Stir in corn, lemon peel, basil leaves, onion powder, salt and pepper. Mix well. Re-cover. Microwave at High for 1 to 2 minutes, or until hot. Add salmon steaks. Spoon pepper mixture over salmon. Re-cover. Microwave at 70% (Medium High) for 14 to 18 minutes, or until fish flakes easily with fork.

With spatula, carefully remove salmon from casserole. Cover to keep warm. Sprinkle flour over vegetable mixture in casserole. Mix well. Blend in half-and-half. Microwave at High for 3 to 4 minutes, or until mixture is slightly thickened, stirring once. Serve pepper mixture with salmon steaks.

Per Serving: Calories: 350 • Protein: 32 g. • Carbohydrate: 15 g. • Fat: 19 g.
• Cholesterol: 90 mg. • Sodium: 410 mg.
Exchanges: ½ starch, 4 lean meat, 1½ vegetable, 1 fat

Crispy Bacon-flavored Fish Fillets

2 tablespoons margarine or butter
1 tablespoon frozen orange juice concentrate, defrosted
1 cup bacon-flavored cracker crumbs (about 20 crackers)
2 teaspoons dried parsley flakes
1 lb. sole fillets, ¼ to ½ inch thick, cut into serving-size pieces

4 servings

Heat conventional oven to 400°F. In shallow dish, microwave margarine at High for 45 seconds to 1 minute, or until melted. Add concentrate. Mix well. In another shallow dish, combine cracker crumbs and parsley flakes.

Dip each side of fillets in margarine mixture, then in crumb mixture, coating well. Place on baking sheet. Bake for 12 to 15 minutes, or until fish flakes easily with fork.

Per Serving: Calories: 240 • Protein: 23 g.
• Carbohydrate: 14 g. • Fat: 10 g.
• Cholesterol: 55 mg. • Sodium: 350 mg.
Exchanges: 1 starch, 3 lean meat

BLT Fish Sandwich ▲

1 recipe Crispy Bacon-flavored Fish Fillets (right)
8 slices bacon
4 hoagie buns

Leaf lettuce
8 tomato slices
4 tablespoons Light & Lean Tartar Sauce (page 106)

4 sandwiches

Prepare fillets as directed. Set aside. Layer 3 paper towels on a plate. Arrange 4 slices of bacon on paper towels. Cover with another paper towel. Microwave at High for 3 to 6 minutes, or until bacon is brown and crisp. Repeat with remaining 4 slices of bacon. Set aside. Cut each bun in half crosswise. Place bottom half of each bun on serving plate. Layer each sandwich with lettuce, 2 tomato slices, 1 fillet, 1 tablespoon of tartar sauce and 2 bacon slices. Top with remaining bun half.

Per Serving: Calories: 470 • Protein: 31 g. • Carbohydrate: 38 g. • Fat: 22 g.
• Cholesterol: 72 mg. • Sodium: 830 mg.
Exchanges: 2 starch, 3 lean meat, 1½ vegetable, 2½ fat

BLT Fish Salad

½ cup sour cream
1 tablespoon frozen orange
   juice concentrate, defrosted
1 tablespoon milk
1 teaspoon sugar
1 recipe Crispy Bacon-
   flavored Fish Fillets (opposite)
8 slices bacon
8 cups torn mixed greens,
   divided (Bibb lettuce, leaf
   lettuce, romaine or spinach)
2 large tomatoes, seeded
   and chopped (2 cups)
1 medium red onion, sliced
   and separated into rings

4 servings

In 2-cup measure, combine
sour cream, concentrate, milk
and sugar. Set dressing aside.
Prepare fillets as directed. Cut
into 1-inch pieces. Set aside.

Layer 3 paper towels on a plate.
Arrange 4 slices of bacon on
paper towels. Cover with another paper towel. Microwave at
High for 3 to 6 minutes, or until
bacon is brown and crisp. Repeat with remaining 4 slices of
bacon. Crumble. Set aside.

On each of 4 individual serving
plates, arrange 2 cups greens,
½ cup tomatoes and one-fourth
of onion slices. Top with one-
fourth of fish and crumbled
bacon. Top each salad with 2
tablespoons of dressing.

Per Serving: Calories: 440 • Protein: 31 g.
• Carbohydrate: 28 g. • Fat: 23 g.
• Cholesterol: 79 mg. • Sodium: 610 mg.
Exchanges: 1 starch, 3½ lean meat,
2½ vegetable, 2½ fat

Start with One Pound of Shrimp or Scallops

For days when you have no time to shop and little time to cook, keep a supply of frozen cooked shrimp in your freezer. Combined with other foods you keep on hand, they make quick-and-easy meals. Fresh shrimp and scallops cook quickly for elegant main dishes. Use them on the day of purchase.

Lightly Coated Shrimp or Scallops

1 lb. medium shrimp, shelled and deveined, or 1 lb. sea scallops
¼ cup cornstarch
¼ cup sesame oil or vegetable oil

How to Make Lightly Coated Shrimp or Scallops

Combine shrimp or scallops and cornstarch in large food-storage bag. Shake to coat shrimp. In 10-inch skillet, heat oil conventionally over medium-high heat.

Add shrimp. Fry for 8 to 10 minutes, or until shrimp are golden brown, stirring frequently. Remove from skillet with slotted spoon. Drain on paper towel.

◄ Shrimp Pasta Oriental

¼ cup sesame seed
1 recipe Lightly Coated Shrimp (above)
8 oz. uncooked linguine
1 tablespoon packed brown sugar
1 tablespoon cornstarch
¼ cup sesame oil
2 tablespoons soy sauce
2 tablespoons sherry
2 tablespoons rice wine vinegar
1 clove garlic, minced
1 cup red pepper chunks (1-inch chunks)
½ cup sliced green onions

4 servings

Heat conventional oven to 350°F. Place sesame seed on baking sheet. Toast for 15 minutes, or until golden brown. Set aside. Prepare shrimp as directed. Set aside. Prepare linguine as directed on package. Rinse and drain. Place in large mixing bowl or salad bowl. Set aside.

In 2-cup measure, combine sugar and cornstarch. Blend in oil, soy sauce, sherry, vinegar and garlic. Stir in red pepper chunks. Microwave at High for 5 to 7 minutes, or until mixture is thickened and translucent, stirring once. Stir in onions. Add soy mixture, sesame seed and shrimp to linguine. Toss to coat.

Variation:
Shrimp Salad Oriental: Follow recipe above, except substitute 8 cups torn mixed greens (Bibb lettuce, leaf lettuce, romaine or spinach) for linguine.

Per Serving: Calories: 660 • Protein: 33 g. • Carbohydrate: 56 g. • Fat: 35 g. • Cholesterol: 173 mg. • Sodium: 690 mg.
Exchanges: 3½ starch, 3 lean meat, ½ vegetable, 5 fat

Garlic Cream-sauced Shrimp

1 whole bulb garlic (2-inch diameter)
  Olive oil
8 oz. uncooked spinach fettucini
2 tablespoons margarine or butter
1 teaspoon grated lemon peel
¼ teaspoon dried oregano leaves
¼ cup all-purpose flour
¼ teaspoon salt
2 cups milk
1 lb. medium shrimp, shelled and deveined
1 medium tomato, seeded and chopped

4 servings

Heat conventional oven to 400°F. Lightly brush outside of garlic bulb with oil. Place in shallow baking pan. Roast on center rack for 30 minutes. Set aside to cool. Prepare fettucini as directed on package. Rinse and drain. Set aside.

In 2-quart casserole, combine margarine, lemon peel and oregano. Remove and discard peel from garlic cloves. Mash garlic, using fork. Add to margarine mixture. Cover. Microwave at High for 1½ to 2½ minutes, or until margarine is melted. Stir in flour and salt. Blend in milk. Microwave at High, uncovered, for 7 to 8 minutes, or until mixture thickens and bubbles, stirring every 2 minutes.

Add shrimp to mixture. Microwave at 70% (Medium High) for 5 to 7½ minutes, or until shrimp are firm and opaque, stirring twice. Stir in half of chopped tomato. Serve shrimp mixture over fettucini. Sprinkle with remaining tomato.

Per Serving: Calories: 470 • Protein: 35 g.
• Carbohydrate: 56 g. • Fat: 11 g.
• Cholesterol: 182 mg. • Sodium: 435 mg.
Exchanges: 3 starch, 3 lean meat,
1 vegetable, ½ low-fat milk

Scallops & Peppers in Red Pepper Sauce ▲

2 medium red peppers, cut into strips (2 cups), divided
1 tablespoon sugar
1 tablespoon margarine or butter
½ teaspoon paprika
⅛ to ¼ teaspoon cayenne

¼ cup whipping cream
1 recipe Lightly Coated Scallops (page 113)
1 medium green pepper, cut into strips (1 cup)
1 medium yellow pepper, cut into strips (1 cup)

6 servings

In 1-quart casserole, combine 1½ cups red pepper strips, the sugar, margarine, paprika and cayenne. Cover. Microwave at High for 12 to 16 minutes, or until pepper strips are tender, stirring once or twice. Spoon mixture into blender. Process until smooth. Add whipping cream. Process until well blended. Set aside. Prepare scallops as directed, except add remaining ½ cup red pepper strips and the green and yellow pepper strips with scallops to 10-inch skillet. Spoon ¼ cup red pepper sauce onto each serving plate. Arrange scallops and peppers evenly over sauce.

Per Serving: Calories: 240 • Protein: 13 g. • Carbohydrate: 12 g. • Fat: 15 g.
• Cholesterol: 39 mg. • Sodium: 150 mg.
Exchanges: 2 lean meat, 2½ vegetable, 2 fat

Scallop & Melon Salad ▲

½ cantaloupe, cut into small chunks (2 cups)
½ honeydew melon, cut into small chunks
   (2 cups)
¼ cup olive oil
3 tablespoons fresh lemon juice
2 tablespoons snipped fresh parsley
1 tablespoon finely chopped fresh jalapeño
   pepper
¼ teaspoon freshly ground pepper
6 slices bacon, chopped
1 lb. bay scallops

4 servings

In medium mixing bowl or salad bowl, combine cantaloupe and honeydew. Set aside. In 1-cup measure, combine oil, lemon juice, parsley, jalapeño pepper and pepper. Add to melon mixture. Toss to coat. Cover with plastic wrap. Chill while preparing remaining ingredients. Place bacon in 10-inch square casserole. Cover with paper towel. Microwave at High for 8 to 12 minutes, or until bacon is brown and crisp. Remove bacon with slotted spoon. Set aside. Add scallops to casserole. Cover. Microwave at 70% (Medium High) for 5 to 8 minutes, or until scallops are opaque, stirring once to rearrange. Drain. Add scallops and bacon to melon mixture. Toss to coat.

Per Serving: Calories: 380 • Protein: 23 g. • Carbohydrate: 25 g.
• Fat: 23 g. • Cholesterol: 49 mg. • Sodium: 360 mg.
Exchanges: 3 lean meat, 1½ fruit, 3 fat

Shrimp & Vegetable Spoon Bread

2 cups frozen broccoli cuts
1 cup frozen corn
1 tablespoon diced pimiento, drained
¼ cup margarine or butter
2½ cups hot water
1½ cups yellow cornmeal
1 teaspoon salt
1 lb. frozen cooked medium shrimp,
   defrosted and drained
1½ cups buttermilk
1 egg, beaten
½ teaspoon pepper

6 servings

Heat conventional oven to 350°F. Grease 13 × 9-inch baking dish. Set aside. Place vegetables in 2-quart casserole. Cover. Microwave at High for 5 to 7 minutes, or until broccoli and corn are defrosted, stirring once. Drain. Set aside. In small bowl, microwave margarine at High for 1¼ to 1½ minutes, or until melted. Set aside. In 8-cup measure, combine water, cornmeal and salt. Microwave at High for 3 to 5 minutes, or until mixture is very thick but can still be stirred smooth, stirring twice with whisk. Add vegetables, margarine and remaining ingredients. Mix well. Pour into prepared dish. Bake conventionally for 45 to 50 minutes, or until mixture is set.

Per Serving: Calories: 320 • Protein: 23 g. • Carbohydrate: 34 g.
• Fat: 11 g. • Cholesterol: 185 mg. • Sodium: 712 mg.
Exchanges: 2 starch, 2 lean meat, 1 vegetable, 1 fat

Shrimp Cakes with New Orleans Remoulade ▲

Sauce:
- 1/3 cup chopped celery
- 1/3 cup chopped onion
- 1/3 cup chopped green pepper
- 1/4 cup mayonnaise
- 3 tablespoons catsup
- 1 tablespoon horseradish
- 1 teaspoon lemon juice
- 1/8 teaspoon cayenne

- 2 tablespoons margarine or butter

- 1 lb. frozen cooked shrimp, defrosted, drained and chopped
- 3/4 cup saltine cracker crumbs
- 2 eggs, beaten
- 1/2 cup sliced green onions
- 1/3 cup frozen corn
- 1/2 teaspoon dry mustard
- 1/4 teaspoon dried thyme leaves
- 1 cup unseasoned dry bread crumbs
  Vegetable oil

6 servings

In 1-quart casserole, combine celery, onion and green pepper. Cover. Microwave at High for 1½ to 2½ minutes, or until vegetables are tender-crisp, stirring once. Add remaining sauce ingredients. Mix well. Set aside. In medium mixing bowl, microwave margarine at High for 45 seconds to 1 minute, or until melted. Add remaining ingredients, except bread crumbs and oil. Mix well. Shape mixture into six 3-inch patties. Place bread crumbs in shallow dish. Dredge both sides of each patty in crumbs, pressing lightly to coat. In 10-inch skillet, heat 1/8 inch oil conventionally over medium-high heat. Fry 3 patties at a time for about 5 minutes, or until deep golden brown, turning over once. Drain on paper-towel-lined plate. Serve with sauce.

Per Serving: Calories: 370 • Protein: 22 g. • Carbohydrate: 26 g. • Fat: 20 g.
• Cholesterol: 225 mg. • Sodium: 620 mg.
Exchanges: 1 starch, 2 lean meat, 2 vegetable, 3 fat

Crunchy Thai Salad

- 2 cups fresh pea pods
- 1/4 cup water
- 1 lb. frozen cooked medium shrimp, defrosted and drained
- 3 cups shredded green cabbage
- 3 cups shredded red cabbage
- 1 cup shredded carrots
- 1/2 cup sliced green onions
- 1 pkg. (3 oz.) chicken-flavored Oriental dry noodle soup mix (discard seasoning packet)

Dressing:
- 1/4 cup creamy peanut butter
- 1/4 cup water
- 3 tablespoons red wine vinegar
- 2 tablespoons vegetable oil
- 1 tablespoon sugar
- 1 teaspoon sesame oil
- 1/4 teaspoon salt
- 1/4 teaspoon pepper

4 to 6 servings

In 2-quart casserole, place pea pods and water. Cover. Microwave at High for 2 to 3 minutes, or until pea pods are very hot and color brightens. Drain.

In large mixing bowl or salad bowl, combine pea pods, shrimp, green and red cabbage, carrots and onions. Break dry noodles into small pieces. Add to salad. Set aside.

In 2-cup measure, combine dressing ingredients. Microwave at High for 2 to 3 minutes, or until dressing can be stirred smooth, stirring twice. Pour over salad. Toss gently to coat. Serve immediately.

Per Serving: Calories: 280 • Protein: 23 g.
• Carbohydrate: 23 g. • Fat: 12 g.
• Cholesterol: 159 mg. • Sodium: 336 mg.
Exchanges: ½ starch, 2 lean meat, 3 vegetable, 1 fat

Shrimp & Spinach Strudel

- 1 pkg. (10 oz.) frozen chopped spinach
- 1 pkg. (8 oz.) cream cheese
- ½ cup sliced almonds
- ⅓ cup sliced green onions
- ¼ teaspoon salt
- ¼ teaspoon pepper
- ¼ teaspoon ground nutmeg
- 1 egg, beaten
- ¼ cup all-purpose flour
- 1 lb. frozen cooked small shrimp, defrosted and drained
- ½ cup margarine or butter
- 12 sheets frozen phyllo dough (18 × 14-inch sheets), defrosted

6 servings

Per Serving: Calories: 470 • Protein: 25 g.
• Carbohydrate: 19 g. • Fat: 34 g.
• Cholesterol: 225 mg. • Sodium: 653 mg.
Exchanges: ½ starch, 2½ lean meat,
2 vegetable, 5½ fat

How to Make Shrimp & Spinach Strudel

Heat conventional oven to 375°F. Place spinach in 2-quart casserole. Cover. Microwave at High for 4 to 6 minutes, or until defrosted. Drain, pressing to remove excess moisture.

Add cream cheese, almonds, onions, salt, pepper and nutmeg. Microwave at High, uncovered, for 1½ to 4 minutes, or until cream cheese is softened. Mix well.

Stir in egg and flour. Add shrimp. Mix well. Set aside. In small mixing bowl, microwave margarine at High for 1½ to 1¾ minutes, or until melted.

Unroll phyllo sheets. Working quickly, place 1 sheet of phyllo on work surface. Brush lightly with margarine. Top with another sheet of phyllo. Brush lightly with margarine.

Repeat with remaining sheets of phyllo, forming layers. Spoon filling lengthwise down center of phyllo sheets to within 2 inches of short ends and 4 inches of long sides.

Fold phyllo over filling. Fold edges under to seal. Place strudel seam-side-down on baking sheet. Bake for 25 to 30 minutes, or until golden brown.

117

Start with Canned Tuna

Canned tuna belongs in everyone's emergency pantry. Use it to create quick, easy and inexpensive dishes from ingredients you keep on hand. Imagination provides unexpected uses for tuna, such as egg rolls or chowder, and fresh approaches to old favorites like salads and casseroles. For additional variety, try the same dishes substituting boneless, skinless salmon for tuna.

◀ Mediterranean Tuna Salad

- 8 oz. uncooked fettucini
- ½ cup red onion wedges, about ¼ inch thick
- 1 clove garlic, minced
- ¼ cup olive oil, divided
- 1 medium zucchini, sliced (1½ cups)
- ¼ cup red wine vinegar
- 1 teaspoon sugar
- 1 teaspoon dried basil leaves
- ¼ teaspoon salt
- ⅛ teaspoon pepper
- 1 can (6½ oz.) solid white tuna, water pack, drained and flaked
- 1 cup halved cherry tomatoes
- ½ cup sliced pitted black olives

4 servings

Prepare fettucini as directed on package. Rinse and drain. Set aside. In 2-quart casserole, combine onion, garlic and 2 tablespoons oil. Microwave at High for 2 to 3 minutes, or until onion is tender-crisp, stirring once. Stir in zucchini. Microwave at High for 1 to 3 minutes, or until zucchini is tender-crisp. Set aside.

In small mixing bowl, combine remaining 2 tablespoons oil, the vinegar, sugar, basil, salt and pepper. Add to zucchini mixture. Microwave at High for 1 minute. In large mixing bowl or salad bowl, combine tuna, tomatoes, olives, fettucini and the zucchini mixture. Toss gently. Serve warm or chilled.

Per Serving: Calories: 420 • Protein: 21 g. • Carbohydrate: 49 g. • Fat: 17 g. • Cholesterol: 7 mg. • Sodium: 435 mg.
Exchanges: 2 starch, 1 lean meat, 4 vegetable, 2½ fat

Sour Cream & Dill Sauced Tuna Patties

Patties:
- 2 cans (6½ oz. each) solid white tuna, water pack, drained and flaked
- ⅓ cup cornflake crumbs
- 1 teaspoon dried dill weed
- ½ teaspoon grated lemon peel
- ¼ teaspoon salt
- ⅛ teaspoon pepper
- 2 teaspoons lemon juice
- 2 eggs, beaten

Sauce:
- 2 tablespoons margarine or butter
- 2 tablespoons all-purpose flour
- 1 tablespoon snipped fresh chives
- ½ teaspoon dried dill weed
- ½ teaspoon grated lemon peel
- ¼ teaspoon salt
- ¾ cup milk
- ½ cup sour cream

4 servings

Heat conventional oven to 375°F. In medium mixing bowl, combine all patty ingredients. Shape into 4 patties, about ½ inch thick. Place in greased 10-inch square casserole. Bake conventionally for 20 to 30 minutes, or until firm and golden brown.

In 4-cup measure, microwave margarine at High for 45 seconds to 1 minute, or until melted. Stir in flour, chives, dill weed, lemon peel and salt. Blend in milk. Microwave at High for 3 to 4 minutes, or until mixture thickens and bubbles, stirring once. Add sour cream. Blend until smooth. Serve sauce over tuna patties. Serve in lettuce-lined buns, if desired.

Per Serving: Calories: 330 • Protein: 31 g. • Carbohydrate: 13 g. • Fat: 16 g. • Cholesterol: 138 mg. • Sodium: 780 mg.
Exchanges: 1 starch, 4 lean meat, 1 fat

Basic Cream Sauce

- ¼ cup chopped red or green pepper
- ¼ cup sliced green onions
- 3 tablespoons margarine or butter
- 3 tablespoons all-purpose flour
- ¼ teaspoon salt
- ⅛ teaspoon pepper
- 1¾ cups milk or half-and-half

Combine red pepper, onions and margarine in 8-cup measure. Microwave at High for 2 to 3 minutes, or until vegetables are tender-crisp, stirring once. Stir in flour, salt and pepper; blend in milk. Microwave at High for 5 to 8 minutes, or until mixture thickens and bubbles, stirring once or twice.

Cheese & Asparagus Creamed Tuna ▲

- 1 recipe Basic Cream Sauce (above)
- 1 pkg. (9 oz.) frozen asparagus cuts
- 1 can (6½ oz.) solid white tuna, water pack, drained and flaked
- 1 pkg. (8 oz.) pasteurized process cheese loaf, shredded
- 1 can (8 oz.) sliced water chestnuts, rinsed and drained
- 4 baked potatoes (page 147)
- ½ cup cooked crumbled bacon

4 servings

Prepare sauce as directed. Set aside. Make slit in asparagus pouch. Place on plate in microwave oven slit-side-up. Microwave at High for 2 to 3 minutes, or until defrosted. Drain. Add tuna and asparagus to thickened sauce. Microwave at High for 2 to 3 minutes, or until hot, stirring once. Stir in cheese and water chestnuts. Microwave at High for 2 to 3 minutes, or until cheese is melted. Slash each potato lengthwise and then crosswise. Gently press both ends until center pops open. Spoon tuna mixture evenly over baked potatoes. Sprinkle with bacon.

Per Serving: Calories: 730 • Protein: 38 g. • Carbohydrate: 78 g. • Fat: 31 g. • Cholesterol: 60 mg. • Sodium: 1480 mg. Exchanges: 3½ starch, 2 lean meat, 4 vegetable, ½ low-fat milk, 4½ fat

Classic Creamed Tuna

- 1 recipe Basic Cream Sauce (above)
- 2 teaspoons prepared horseradish
- 1 can (6½ oz.) solid white tuna, water pack, drained and flaked
- 1 cup frozen peas
- 2 hard-cooked eggs, chopped, divided
- 4 slices bread, toasted and cut diagonally into quarters
- 1 tablespoon snipped fresh parsley

4 servings

Prepare sauce as directed, adding horseradish with flour. After sauce thickens, stir in tuna, peas and half of chopped eggs. Microwave at High for 2 to 3 minutes, or until hot, stirring once. Serve over toast points. Sprinkle with remaining hard-cooked eggs and the parsley.

Serving suggestion: Omit toast points and serve tuna mixture over baked patty shells, hot mashed potatoes or hot pasta. Sprinkle with snipped fresh parsley or grated Parmesan cheese.

Per Serving: Calories: 330 • Protein: 23 g. • Carbohydrate: 28 g. • Fat: 15 g. • Cholesterol: 122 mg. • Sodium: 615 mg. Exchanges: 1½ starch, 2½ lean meat, 1 vegetable, 1 fat

Oriental Tuna Frittata

- 6 eggs, beaten
- ¼ teaspoon ground ginger
- ¼ teaspoon salt
- 2 tablespoons milk
- 1 can (6½ oz.) solid white tuna, water pack, drained and flaked
- 2 tablespoons margarine or butter, divided
- ¼ cup chopped carrot
- ¼ cup chopped green pepper
- 1 cup sliced fresh mushrooms
- 1 tablespoon plus 1 teaspoon sugar
- 1 tablespoon cornstarch
- ¼ teaspoon ground ginger
- ¼ teaspoon garlic powder
- ⅛ teaspoon cayenne
- ¼ cup soy sauce
- ¼ cup water

4 servings

In medium mixing bowl, combine eggs, ginger, salt and milk. Stir in tuna. Set aside. In 9-inch skillet, melt 1 tablespoon margarine conventionally over medium heat. Stir in carrot and green pepper. Cook and stir for 2 to 4 minutes, or until vegetables are tender-crisp. Add mushrooms. Cook and stir for 1 to 2 minutes, or until mushrooms are tender. Remove vegetables from skillet. Set aside.

Melt remaining 1 tablespoon margarine in skillet. Reduce heat to low. Add egg mixture. Cover. Cook over low heat for 12 to 15 minutes, or until eggs are set. Spread vegetables evenly over eggs. Re-cover and remove from heat. In 2-cup measure, combine remaining ingredients. Microwave at High for 2 to 3 minutes, or until mixture is thickened and translucent, stirring once. Serve sauce over frittata.

Per Serving: Calories: 260 • Protein: 23 g.
• Carbohydrate: 11 g. • Fat: 14 g.
• Cholesterol: 328 mg. • Sodium: 1490 mg.
Exchanges: 2½ lean meat, 2 vegetable, 1½ fat

Tuna Cobb Salad

½ cup white wine vinegar
¼ cup olive oil
1 clove garlic, minced
1 teaspoon sugar
½ teaspoon dried marjoram
   leaves
¼ teaspoon salt
¼ teaspoon dry mustard
1 can (6½ oz.) solid white
   tuna, water pack, drained
8 slices bacon, cut into
   2-inch pieces
1 head Bibb lettuce
1 tomato, cut into thin wedges
3 hard-cooked eggs, sliced
1 avocado, peeled and sliced
¼ cup crumbled blue cheese

4 servings

In 2-cup measure, combine vinegar, oil, garlic, sugar, marjoram, salt and mustard. Microwave at High for 2 to 2½ minutes, or until mixture just begins to boil. Place tuna in small mixing bowl. Spoon 3 to 4 tablespoons dressing mixture over tuna. Cover with plastic wrap. Chill 1 hour. Set remaining dressing aside.

Place bacon pieces in 1½-quart casserole. Cover with paper towel. Microwave at High for 6 to 8 minutes, or until bacon is brown and crisp, stirring once. Drain on paper towel. On large serving platter, arrange lettuce. Top with tomato, eggs, avocado, tuna and bacon. Sprinkle with blue cheese. Serve with remaining dressing.

Per Serving: Calories: 430 • Protein: 24 g. • Carbohydrate: 10 g. • Fat: 34 g.
• Cholesterol: 183 mg. • Sodium: 655 mg.
Exchanges: 3 lean meat, 2 vegetable, 5 fat

Corn Bread Topped Tuna Casserole ▶

Casserole:
- 3 tablespoons margarine or butter
- 3 tablespoons all-purpose flour
- ¼ teaspoon onion powder
- ¼ teaspoon dried thyme leaves
- 1½ cups milk
- ½ teaspoon Worcestershire sauce
- 1½ cups frozen mixed corn, broccoli and red pepper
- ½ cup shredded Monterey Jack cheese
- 1 can (6½ oz.) solid white tuna, water pack, drained and flaked

Topping:
- 2 tablespoons margarine or butter
- ¾ cup yellow cornmeal
- ¼ cup all-purpose flour
- 1 tablespoon sugar
- 2 teaspoons baking powder
- ¼ teaspoon salt
- ¼ teaspoon onion powder
- ½ cup milk
- 1 egg, beaten

4 servings

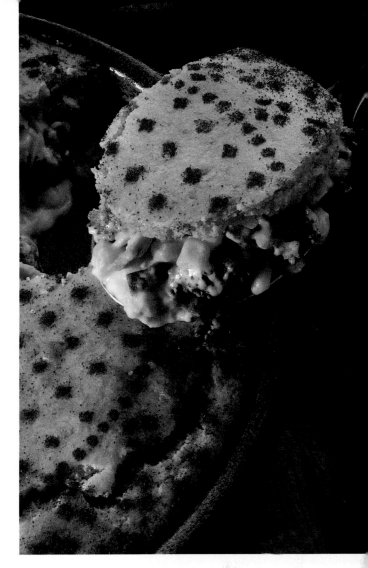

Heat conventional oven to 400°F. In 4-cup measure, microwave 3 tablespoons margarine at High for 1 to 1¼ minutes, or until melted. Stir in 3 tablespoons flour, ¼ teaspoon onion powder and the thyme. Blend in 1½ cups milk and the Worcestershire sauce. Microwave at High for 4 to 6 minutes, or until mixture thickens and bubbles, stirring twice. Stir in vegetables, cheese and tuna. Spread evenly in 9-inch round cake dish. Set aside.

In small bowl, microwave 2 tablespoons margarine at High for 45 seconds to 1 minute, or until melted. Set aside. In medium mixing bowl, combine remaining ingredients, except milk and egg. Stir in milk and egg until blended. Blend in melted margarine. Spoon batter evenly over tuna mixture. Bake conventionally for 12 to 16 minutes, or until light golden brown.

Serving suggestion: To decorate casserole after baking, place doily over top; sprinkle with paprika. Remove doily.

Per Serving: Calories: 480 • Protein: 26 g. • Carbohydrate: 44 g. • Fat: 24 g. • Cholesterol: 82 mg. • Sodium: 770 mg.
Exchanges: 2 starch, 2 lean meat, 3 vegetable, 3 fat

Cheesy Tuna & Rice Casserole

- 2 cups frozen broccoli cuts
- 1½ cups uncooked instant rice
- 1 jar (2 oz.) diced pimiento, drained
- ½ teaspoon dried dill weed
- ¼ teaspoon salt
- ¼ teaspoon onion powder
- 1½ cups water
- 1 can (6½ oz.) solid white tuna, water pack, drained and flaked
- 1½ cups shredded Cheddar cheese

4 to 6 servings

In 3-quart casserole, combine all ingredients, except tuna and cheese. Cover. Microwave at High for 4 minutes. Stir in tuna. Re-cover. Microwave at High for 3 to 6 minutes, or until rice is tender and liquid is absorbed. Stir in cheese. Re-cover. Microwave at High for 1 to 3 minutes, or until cheese is melted, stirring once. Let stand, covered, for 5 minutes.

Per Serving: Calories: 250 • Protein: 18 g. • Carbohydrate: 22 g. • Fat: 10 g. • Cholesterol: 35 mg. • Sodium: 375 mg.
Exchanges: 1 starch, 2 lean meat, 1½ vegetable, ½ fat

Easy Bread Bowls

1 pkg. (10 oz.) refrigerated hot
   loaf dough
1 tablespoon margarine or
   butter

Sprinkle with: sesame
   seed, poppy seed, instant
   minced onion, garlic
   powder or dried herbs

How to Make
Easy Bread Bowls

Grease jelly roll pan. Grease the
outsides of four 6-oz. custard
cups. Invert onto prepared pan.
Set aside. Heat conventional
oven to 350°F. Remove dough
from package. Cut crosswise
into 4 pieces. With greased
hands, press each piece into
5-inch round.

Press each round over outside
of prepared custard cup. In
small bowl, microwave margarine at High for 45 seconds to
1 minute, or until melted. Brush
evenly over dough. Sprinkle
with desired seasoning.

Bake conventionally for 16 to 20
minutes, or until golden brown.
Loosen edges. Carefully remove
bread bowls from custard cups.
Serve warm, filled with thick,
hearty soups or salads.

Curried Tuna Crunch Salad ▲

1 recipe Easy Bread Bowls
   (right)

Salad:
3 cups cooked long-grain
   white rice
1 cup sliced celery
1 medium red apple, cored
   and chopped
1 can (6½ oz.) solid white
   tuna, water pack, drained
   and flaked
½ cup slivered almonds
⅓ cup raisins

Dressing:
½ cup mayonnaise or salad
   dressing
½ cup sour cream
2 tablespoons milk
1 tablespoon curry powder
½ teaspoon salt
¼ teaspoon garlic powder

4 servings

Prepare bread bowls as directed. Set aside. In large mixing bowl
or salad bowl, combine all salad ingredients. In small mixing bowl,
combine all dressing ingredients. Add dressing to salad. Toss to
coat. Serve in bread bowls. Top with one or more of the following, if
desired: chopped hard-cooked egg, cooked crumbled bacon, sliced
green onions or chopped red pepper.

Per Serving: Calories: 890 • Protein: 27 g. • Carbohydrate: 99 g. • Fat: 44 g.
• Cholesterol: 41 mg. • Sodium: 1010 mg.
Exchanges: 5 starch, 1 lean meat, 1½ vegetable, 1 fruit, 8 fat

Tuna Potato Chowder

1 recipe Easy Bread Bowls (opposite)
½ cup sliced green onions
1 tablespoon margarine or butter
2 cups frozen mixed broccoli, cauliflower and carrots
1 can (14½ oz.) ready-to-serve chicken broth
1 can (10¾ oz.) condensed cream of potato soup
¼ teaspoon dried oregano leaves
⅛ teaspoon pepper
2 tablespoons all-purpose flour
½ cup milk
1 can (6½ oz.) solid white tuna, water pack, drained and flaked

4 servings

Prepare bread bowls as directed. Set aside. In 3-quart casserole, combine onions and margarine. Microwave at High for 2 to 3 minutes, or until onions are tender, stirring once. Stir in vegetables. Microwave at High for 2 to 2½ minutes, or until defrosted, stirring once to break apart. Stir in broth, soup, oregano and pepper. Cover. Microwave at High for 10 to 14 minutes, or until mixture is hot and begins to boil, stirring once or twice.

In small mixing bowl, combine flour and milk, blending until smooth. Add flour mixture and tuna to soup. Re-cover. Microwave at High for 3 to 5 minutes, or until soup thickens and bubbles. Serve in bread bowls.

Per Serving: Calories: 410 • Protein: 25 g.
• Carbohydrate: 48 g. • Fat: 13 g.
• Cholesterol: 14 mg. • Sodium: 1610 mg.
Exchanges: 2½ starch, 2 lean meat, 2 vegetable, 1½ fat

Crispy Tuna Egg Rolls ▲

1 cup sliced celery
1 cup fresh bean sprouts
⅓ cup sliced green onions
1 tablespoon margarine or butter
1 cup shredded Cheddar cheese
1 can (6½ oz.) solid white tuna, water pack, drained and flaked
1 teaspoon dry mustard
¼ teaspoon garlic powder
8 egg roll skins (7-inch)
1 egg white
Vegetable oil
½ cup mayonnaise or salad dressing
1 tablespoon sweet hot mustard

4 servings

In 2-quart casserole, combine celery, bean sprouts, onions and margarine. Cover. Microwave at High for 5 to 6 minutes, or until celery is tender-crisp, stirring once. Add cheese, tuna, dry mustard and garlic powder. Mix well. Spoon about ⅓ cup tuna mixture diagonally across 1 egg roll skin, just below center. Roll up, folding in sides. Brush top corner with egg white; continue rolling to complete seal. Repeat with remaining egg roll skins.

In deep 10-inch skillet, heat ½ inch vegetable oil conventionally over medium-high heat. Fry 4 egg rolls at a time for about 5 minutes, or until golden brown, turning 2 or 3 times. Drain on paper towels. In small mixing bowl, combine mayonnaise and sweet hot mustard. Serve with egg rolls.

Per Serving: Calories: 640 • Protein: 26 g. • Carbohydrate: 22 g. • Fat: 50 g.
• Cholesterol: 54 mg. • Sodium: 1010 mg.
Exchanges: 1 starch, 3 lean meat, 1 vegetable, 8 fat

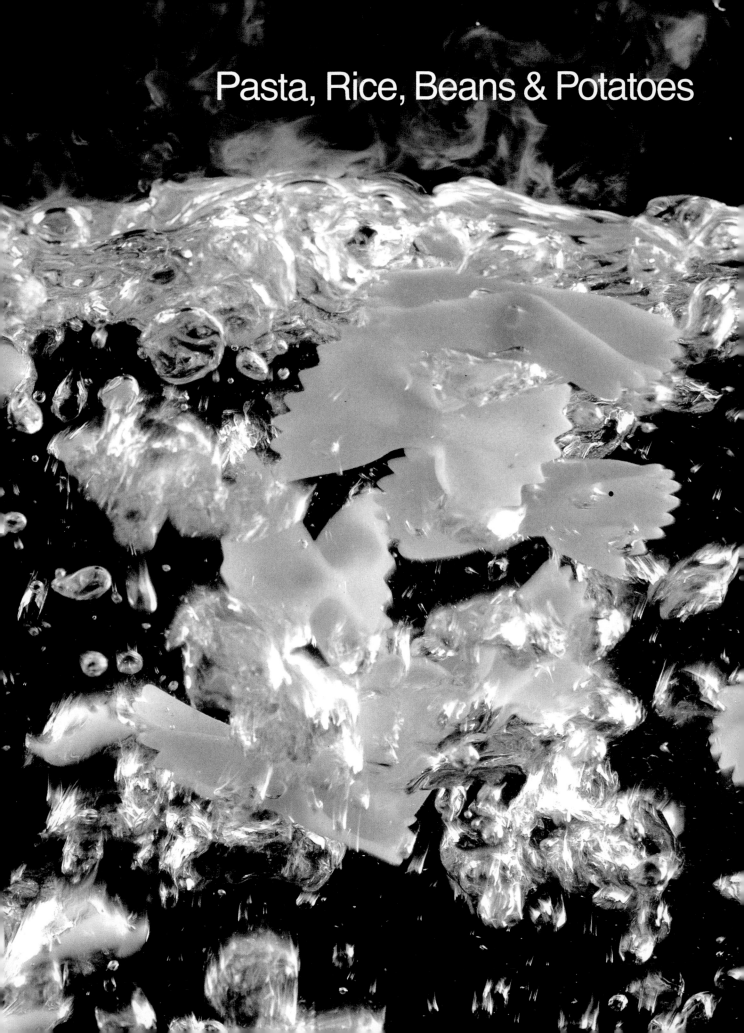

Pasta, Rice, Beans & Potatoes

VERMICELLI EXTRA THIN SPAGHETTI
NET WT. 7 OZ.
Cooks in 5 minutes
ENRICHED

Start with One Package of Pasta

Count on pasta for variety in vegetarian dishes. Serve it hot or cold, al dente or crisply fried. Sauce it with imagination in a jewel-like mixture of colorful vegetables, a creamy, out-of-the-ordinary cheese sauce, lightly curried or sassy with spice. If you buy bulk pasta, weigh or measure it to obtain the amounts called for in the recipes.

Crispy Pasta Cake

1 pkg. (7 oz.) uncooked capellini (angel hair spaghetti) or vermicelli
3 tablespoons vegetable oil, divided
1 clove garlic, minced (optional)

How to Make Crispy Pasta Cake

Prepare pasta as directed on package. Rinse and drain. Place pasta in large mixing bowl. Add 1 tablespoon oil. Toss to coat. Set aside.

Heat remaining 2 tablespoons oil in 10-inch nonstick skillet over medium-high heat. Add garlic and pasta, pressing into an even layer. Cook for about 4 to 5 minutes, or until golden brown.

◄ Szechuan-sauced Pasta Cake

1 recipe Crispy Pasta Cake (above)
8 oz. fresh mushrooms, cut in half (2 cups)
2 medium carrots, cut into julienne strips (2 × 1/4-inch strips)
2 cups fresh bean sprouts
4 oz. fresh pea pods
1/2 cup sliced green onions
1 tablespoon cornstarch
1/4 to 1/2 teaspoon crushed red pepper flakes
1/3 cup water
1/4 cup prepared stir-fry sauce
1 pkg. (2 oz.) cashews (optional)

4 servings

Prepare pasta cake. Invert onto 12-inch round serving plate, browned-side-up. Cover to keep warm. In 2-quart casserole, combine mushrooms, carrots, bean sprouts, pea pods and onions. Set aside.

In small mixing bowl, combine cornstarch and red pepper flakes. Blend in water and stir-fry sauce. Pour over vegetables. Toss to coat. Microwave at High, uncovered, for 9 to 16 minutes, or until vegetables are tender and sauce is thickened and translucent, stirring 3 or 4 times. Stir in cashews. Spoon vegetable mixture over pasta cake. Serve in wedges.

Per Serving: Calories: 350 • Protein: 11 g. • Carbohydrate: 53 g. • Fat: 12 g.
• Cholesterol: 0 • Sodium: 710 mg.
Exchanges: 2½ starch, 3 vegetable, 2 fat

Italian-sauced Pasta Cake ▲

1 recipe Crispy Pasta Cake (page 129)
1 cup spaghetti sauce
1 oz. sliced fully cooked pepperoni (¼ cup)
1 cup shredded mozzarella or Co-Jack
  cheese

4 servings

Prepare pasta cake. Invert onto 12-inch round serving plate browned-side-up. Spread sauce over top of pasta cake to within 1 inch of edge. Arrange pepperoni evenly over sauce. Sprinkle with cheese. Microwave at 70% (Medium High) for 6 to 8 minutes, or until pasta cake is hot and cheese is melted, rotating plate twice. Serve in wedges.

Per Serving: Calories: 450 • Protein: 16 g. • Carbohydrate: 46 g.
• Fat: 22 g. • Cholesterol: 21 mg. • Sodium: 600 mg.
Exchanges: 2½ starch, ½ medium-fat meat, 2 vegetable, 4 fat

Fettucini with Gorgonzola & Peas

1 pkg. (16 oz.) uncooked fettucini
½ cup chopped roasted red peppers
1 pkg. (16 oz.) frozen peas
¼ cup water
6 oz. gorgonzola cheese, crumbled (1 cup)
¾ cup half-and-half
¼ teaspoon salt

6 to 8 servings

Prepare fettucini as directed on package. Rinse and drain. Place in large mixing bowl or serving bowl. Add red peppers. Set aside. In 2-quart casserole, combine peas and water. Cover. Microwave at High for 6 to 8 minutes, or until hot, stirring once. Drain. Add to fettucini. Set aside. In 4-cup measure, combine gorgonzola, half-and-half and salt. Microwave at 50% (Medium) for 6 to 9 minutes, or until mixture can be stirred smooth and cheese is melted, stirring twice. Add sauce to fettucini. Toss to combine. Serve immediately.

Per Serving: Calories: 350 • Protein: 15 g. • Carbohydrate: 50 g.
• Fat: 10 g. • Cholesterol: 24 mg. • Sodium: 440 mg.
Exchanges: 3 starch, ½ high-fat meat, 1 vegetable, 1 fat

Curried Noodles with Peppers & Peanuts

1 pkg. (16 oz.) uncooked fine egg noodles
1 medium green pepper, cut into thin strips
1 medium red pepper, cut into thin strips
½ cup sliced green onions
1 tablespoon curry powder
2 teaspoons cornstarch
¼ teaspoon garlic powder
¼ teaspoon crushed red pepper flakes
½ cup ready-to-serve chicken broth
3 tablespoons vegetable oil
½ cup peanuts

6 to 8 servings

Prepare egg noodles as directed on package. Rinse and drain. Set aside.

In 3-quart casserole, combine green and red pepper strips and onions. In small mixing bowl, combine curry powder, cornstarch, garlic powder and red pepper flakes. Blend in broth and oil. Pour over vegetable mixture. Toss to coat.

Microwave at High, uncovered, for 6 to 9 minutes, or until peppers are tender-crisp and sauce is thickened, stirring 2 or 3 times. Stir in peanuts. Add noodles. Toss to coat.

Per Serving: Calories: 350 • Protein: 11 g.
• Carbohydrate: 49 g. • Fat: 12 g.
• Cholesterol: 58 mg. • Sodium: 135 mg.
Exchanges: 3 starch, 1 vegetable, 2 fat

Caesar Pasta Salad

1 pkg. (16 oz.) uncooked
  bow tie pasta
6 cups romaine lettuce, torn
  into bite-size pieces
3 tablespoons margarine or
  butter
2 cloves garlic, minced
3 cups cubed French bread
  (1-inch cubes)
3/4 cup creamy Caesar
  dressing
4 hard-cooked eggs, sliced

8 servings

Prepare pasta as directed on package. Rinse with cold water. Drain. Place in large mixing bowl or salad bowl. Add lettuce. Set aside. In 10-inch square casserole, microwave margarine and garlic at High for 1 to 1¼ minutes, or until margarine is melted. Mix well. Add bread cubes. Toss to coat.

Microwave at High, uncovered, for 6 to 7 minutes, or until bread cubes are crisp, stirring twice. Cool. Add bread cubes and dressing to salad. Toss to coat. Add egg slices. Toss gently to combine. Serve immediately.

Per Serving: Calories: 420 • Protein: 12 g. • Carbohydrate: 55 g. • Fat: 16 g.
• Cholesterol: 112 mg. • Sodium: 340 mg.
Exchanges: 3 starch, ½ medium-fat meat, 2½ fat

Vegetable Lo Mein

1   pkg. (8 oz.) uncooked Chinese noodles
1   tablespoon plus 2 teaspoons cornstarch
⅔ cup ready-to-serve chicken broth
¼ cup soy sauce
¼ cup sherry
2   tablespoons hoisin sauce
1   teaspoon sesame oil
1   clove garlic, minced
¼ teaspoon white pepper
2   cups thinly sliced carrots
2   cups sliced bok choy, stems and leaves
     (1-inch slices)
2   cups julienne cucumbers (1½ × ¼-inch
     strips)
1   cup julienne radishes (1 × ⅛-inch strips)

4 servings

Prepare noodles as directed on package. Rinse and drain. Place in large mixing bowl or serving bowl. Set aside. Place cornstarch in 2-quart casserole. Blend in broth, soy sauce, sherry, hoisin sauce, oil, garlic and pepper. Add carrots. Mix well.

Microwave at High for 6 to 9 minutes, or until sauce is thickened and translucent, stirring twice. Add sauce and remaining ingredients to noodles. Toss to coat. Serve immediately.

Per Serving: Calories: 340 • Protein: 12 g. • Carbohydrate: 60 g.
• Fat: 5 g. • Cholesterol: 58 mg. • Sodium: 1290 mg.
Exchanges: 3 starch, 3 vegetable, 1 fat

Start with One Cup of Rice

Rice can be much more than a bland side dish or the background of an Oriental entrée. Supplemented with nuts, beans or cheese, rice provides the primary protein in lively main dishes.

Cheesy Herbed Brown Rice Crust

Nonstick vegetable
cooking spray
1 cup uncooked brown rice
1 cup shredded mozzarella
cheese
2 egg whites
1 teaspoon dried dill weed

How to Make Cheesy Herbed Brown Rice Crust

Heat conventional oven to 350°F. Spray 12-inch pizza pan or 10-inch deep-dish pie plate with cooking spray. Set aside. Prepare rice as directed on package. Drain. Add cheese, egg whites and dill weed. Mix well.

Press brown rice mixture against bottom of prepared pan, using back of spoon. Bake conventionally for 20 to 22 minutes, or until crust is set and begins to brown.

◄ Vegetable Quiche*

1 recipe Cheesy Herbed
Brown Rice Crust (left)
1 pkg. (16 oz.) frozen
broccoli, cauliflower and
carrots
1/4 cup water
2 eggs, beaten
2 egg yolks, beaten
1/4 cup milk
1 tablespoon all-purpose flour
1/4 teaspoon salt
1/8 teaspoon pepper
1 cup shredded Monterey
Jack cheese
1 cup cottage cheese

4 to 6 servings

Prepare crust as directed, pressing mixture into 10-inch deep-dish pie plate. Set aside. In 2-quart casserole, combine vegetables and water. Cover. Microwave at High for 6 to 8 minutes, or until defrosted, stirring once. Drain. Coarsely chop vegetables. Set aside.

In medium mixing bowl, combine eggs, egg yolks, milk, flour, salt and pepper. Add vegetables and cheeses. Mix well. Pour into prepared crust. Cover with wax paper. Microwave at 70% (Medium High) for 18 to 23 minutes, or until center is set, rotating twice. Let stand for 5 minutes.

*Recipe not recommended for ovens with less than 600 cooking watts.

Per Serving: Calories: 360 • Protein: 23 g.
• Carbohydrate: 32 g. • Fat: 15 g.
• Cholesterol: 177 mg. • Sodium: 520 mg.
Exchanges: 1 starch, 2 medium-fat meat, 3 vegetable, 1 fat

Rice-crusted Vegetable Pizza

1 recipe Cheesy Herbed
Brown Rice Crust (left)
1 can (8 oz.) tomato sauce
1 teaspoon dried basil leaves
1 teaspoon dried oregano
leaves
1 pkg. (16 oz.) frozen
broccoli, cauliflower and
carrots
1/4 cup water
1 cup shredded mozzarella
cheese

4 servings

Prepare crust as directed, pressing mixture into 12-inch pizza pan. Set aside. In small mixing bowl, combine tomato sauce, basil and oregano. Spoon sauce over crust. Set aside.

In 2-quart casserole, combine vegetables and water. Cover. Microwave at High for 6 to 8 minutes, or until defrosted, stirring once. Drain. Coarsely chop vegetables. Spoon vegetables over sauce. Sprinkle evenly with cheese. Bake conventionally for 12 to 15 minutes, or until pizza is hot and cheese is melted.

Per Serving: Calories: 390 • Protein: 24 g.
• Carbohydrate: 49 g. • Fat: 11 g.
• Cholesterol: 31 mg. • Sodium: 710 mg.
Exchanges: 1½ starch, 1½ medium-fat meat, 5 vegetable, ½ fat

Taco Rice Salad

Vegetable oil
4 flour tortillas (8-inch)
2 cups hot water
1 cup uncooked long-grain
   white rice
1 pkg. (1.25 oz.) taco
   seasoning mix
1 cup chopped avocado
1 cup shredded lettuce
1 cup seeded chopped
   tomato
½ cup sliced black olives
½ cup chopped onion
1 can (4 oz.) chopped green
   chilies, drained
1 can (16 oz.) refried beans
¼ cup shredded Cheddar
   cheese

4 servings

Per Serving: Calories: 610 • Protein: 18 g.
• Carbohydrate: 99 g. • Fat: 17 g.
• Cholesterol: 7 mg. • Sodium: 1600 mg.
Exchanges: 5 starch, 4½ vegetable, 3 fat

How to Make Taco Rice Salad

Invert four 10-oz. custard cups on large baking sheet with sides. Arrange cups at least 3 inches apart on baking sheet. Heat conventional oven to 350°F.

Heat ⅛ inch oil conventionally in 10-inch skillet over medium-high heat. Dip both sides of each tortilla in hot oil to moisten. Drape 1 tortilla over each custard cup.

Bake for 10 to 12 minutes, or until shells begin to brown lightly. Cool completely. Carefully lift tortilla shells off custard cups. Set aside.

Combine water, rice and taco seasoning in 2-quart casserole. Cover. Microwave at High for 5 minutes. Microwave at 50% (Medium) for 12 to 15 minutes longer, or until rice is tender and water is absorbed. Fluff with fork.

Stir in avocado, lettuce, tomato and olives. Mix well. Set aside. In 1-quart casserole, combine onion and chilies. Cover. Microwave at High for 3 to 5 minutes, or until onion is tender, stirring once. Add beans. Mix well.

Microwave at High, uncovered, for 3 to 5 minutes, or until hot, stirring once. Spoon bean mixture evenly into tortilla shells. Spoon rice mixture evenly over bean mixture. Sprinkle each salad with 1 tablespoon cheese.

Three-mushroom Spinach Rissoto

1¾ cups warm water, divided
1 pkg. (0.5 oz.) dried morel
   mushrooms
1½ cups sliced fresh
   mushrooms
1 cup sliced fresh shiitake
   mushrooms
¼ cup chopped onion
2 tablespoons margarine or
   butter
1 can (14½ oz.) ready-to-
   serve chicken broth
1 cup uncooked arborio rice
¼ cup white wine
6 cups torn fresh spinach
   leaves
½ cup shredded fresh
   Parmesan cheese
¼ cup pine nuts

4 servings

In 2-cup measure, combine 1½ cups water and the morels. Let stand for about ½ hour, or until morels are rehydrated. Drain and chop morels.

In 3-quart casserole, combine morel, fresh and shiitake mushrooms, onion and margarine. Cover. Microwave at High for 6 to 8 minutes, or until mushrooms are tender, stirring once.

Add broth, rice, wine and remaining ¼ cup water. Mix well. Microwave at High, uncovered, for 15 to 20 minutes, or until liquid is almost absorbed, stirring 3 or 4 times. Add spinach, cheese and pine nuts. Mix well. Let stand, covered, for 5 minutes.

Per Serving: Calories: 410 • Protein: 19 g.
• Carbohydrate: 50 g. • Fat: 15 g.
• Cholesterol: 11 mg. • Sodium: 1010 mg.
Exchanges: 2 starch, ½ lean meat,
4 vegetable, 2½ fat

Vegetable Jambalaya ▲

1 cup uncooked long-grain
   white rice
1 can (16 oz.) butter beans,
   rinsed and drained
1 can (16 oz.) black-eyed
   peas, rinsed and drained
1 can (15 oz.) whole
   tomatoes, undrained and
   cut up
1 can (14½ oz.) ready-to-serve
   beef broth

1 pkg. (10 oz.) frozen cut okra
1 cup frozen corn
1 cup frozen peas
1 clove garlic, minced
1 teaspoon dried parsley
   flakes
½ teaspoon salt
½ teaspoon dried thyme
   leaves
¼ teaspoon cayenne
¼ teaspoon pepper

6 to 8 servings

In 3-quart casserole, combine all ingredients. Cover. Microwave at High for 20 to 30 minutes, or until liquid is absorbed and mixture is hot, stirring 2 or 3 times. Let stand, covered, for 10 minutes.

Per Serving: Calories: 220 • Protein: 10 g. • Carbohydrate: 45 g. • Fat: 1 g.
• Cholesterol: 0 • Sodium: 410 mg.
Exchanges: 2½ starch, 1 vegetable

Sizzling Rice Soup

- 2 cups hot water
- 1 cup uncooked long-grain white rice
- ½ teaspoon salt
- 2 cups ready-to-serve chicken broth
- 1 pkg. (16 oz.) frozen broccoli, carrots, water chestnuts and red peppers
- ¼ cup chili sauce
- 1 tablespoon soy sauce
- 1 tablespoon white vinegar
- ¼ teaspoon crushed red pepper flakes
- 2 tablespoons margarine or butter
- 2 tablespoons vegetable oil

6 servings

In 2-quart casserole, combine water, rice and salt. Cover. Microwave at High for 5 minutes. Stir. Microwave at 50% (Medium) for 12 to 15 minutes longer, or until rice is tender and water is absorbed, stirring twice. (Stirring is necessary to make rice sticky.) Set aside.

In 3-quart casserole, combine remaining ingredients, except margarine and oil. Cover. Microwave at High for 10 to 15 minutes, or until hot, stirring once. Set aside.

Shape rice into 1-inch balls. In 10-inch nonstick skillet, heat margarine and oil conventionally over medium-high heat. Fry rice balls about 8 to 10 minutes, or until golden brown, turning over several times. Remove from skillet with slotted spoon. Add to soup. Mix well. Serve immediately.

Per Serving: Calories: 250 • Protein: 6 g.
• Carbohydrate: 36 g. • Fat: 9 g.
• Cholesterol: 0 • Sodium: 830 mg.
Exchanges: 1 starch, 4 vegetable, 1½ fat

Start with Canned Beans

Combine canned beans with rice or cheese for a satisfying, nutritious meal from supplies kept on hand in your pantry and refrigerator.

◀ Four-bean Salad

½ lb. fresh green beans, cut into 1½-inch lengths
1 cup sliced celery
¼ cup water
1 can (16 oz.) black-eyed peas, rinsed and drained
1 can (16 oz.) garbanzo beans, rinsed and drained
1 can (16 oz.) kidney beans, rinsed and drained
½ cup chopped red onion
¼ cup plus 2 tablespoons red wine vinegar
¼ cup vegetable oil
1 teaspoon dry mustard
1 teaspoon Worcestershire sauce
1 clove garlic, minced
½ teaspoon salt
¼ teaspoon pepper

6 to 8 servings

In 2-quart casserole, combine green beans, celery and water. Cover. Microwave at High for 6 to 8 minutes, or until beans and celery are bright green, stirring once. Drain. In large mixing bowl or salad bowl, combine green beans and celery with remaining ingredients. Cover. Chill 2 to 3 hours to blend flavors. Serve on bed of lettuce or hot cooked saffron rice, if desired.

Per Serving: Calories: 210 • Protein: 10 g. • Carbohydrate: 29 g. • Fat: 8 g. • Cholesterol: 0 • Sodium: 160 mg. Exchanges: 1½ starch, 1 vegetable, 1½ fat

Black Bean & Ham Soup*▲

4 cups hot water
1 can (28 oz.) whole tomatoes, undrained and cut up
1 ham hock (about 1 lb.)
1½ teaspoons chili powder
2 thin lemon slices
2 cans (16 oz. each) black beans, rinsed and drained

6 to 8 servings

In 5-quart casserole, combine all ingredients, except beans. Cover. Microwave at High for 10 minutes. Microwave at 50% (Medium) for 1 hour longer, turning ham hock over and stirring 3 times. Remove ham hock. Cut ham from bone. Return ham to soup. Discard bone. Add beans. Mix well. Re-cover. Microwave at High for 10 to 15 minutes, or until hot.

*Recipe not recommended for ovens with less than 600 cooking watts.

Per Serving: Calories: 130 • Protein: 10 g. • Carbohydrate: 21 g. • Fat: 1 g. • Cholesterol: 8 mg. • Sodium: 340 mg. Exchanges: 1 starch, ½ lean meat, 1 vegetable

Tomato Chick Pea Soup au Gratin

- 1 medium onion, thinly sliced
- 2 tablespoons margarine or butter
- ½ teaspoon dried basil leaves
- 1 can (15 oz.) garbanzo beans, rinsed and drained
- 1 can (10¾ oz.) condensed tomato soup
- 1½ cups water
- 4 slices French bread (1-inch slices), toasted
- 1½ cups shredded Co-Jack cheese

4 servings

In 2-quart casserole, combine onion, margarine and basil. Cover. Microwave at High for 6 to 9 minutes, or until onion is tender, stirring once or twice.

Add beans, soup and water. Mix well. Cover. Microwave at High for 5 to 6 minutes, or until hot, stirring twice. Ladle soup evenly into four 12-oz. ovenproof soup bowls. Place bowls on large baking sheet. Top each with piece of toast. Sprinkle evenly with cheese.

Place under conventional broiler, 2 to 3 inches from heat. Broil for 3 to 5 minutes, or until cheese is melted. Serve immediately.

Per Serving: Calories: 480 • Protein: 21 g.
• Carbohydrate: 50 g. • Fat: 23 g.
• Cholesterol: 40 mg. • Sodium: 1050 mg.
Exchanges: 2½ starch, 1½ medium-fat meat, 2½ vegetable, 3 fat

Ratatouille & Bean Stew

1 medium eggplant, cut into
  ½-inch cubes
1 can (28 oz.) Roma tomatoes,
  drained and cut up
2 cups sliced zucchini
1 medium green pepper, cut
  into strips
1 medium onion, sliced and
  separated into rings

¼ cup olive oil
2 teaspoons dried parsley
  flakes
1 teaspoon dried oregano
  leaves
1 teaspoon salt
½ teaspoon sugar
1 can (16 oz.) chili beans in
  chili sauce

6 to 8 servings

In 10-inch square casserole,
combine all ingredients, except
beans. Cover. Microwave at
High for 20 to 25 minutes, or until
eggplant is tender and translucent, stirring twice. Add beans.
Mix well. Re-cover. Microwave at
High for 3 to 5 minutes, or until
hot, stirring once.

Per Serving: Calories: 150 • Protein: 5 g.
• Carbohydrate: 15 g. • Fat: 10 g.
• Cholesterol: 10 mg. • Sodium: 575 mg.
Exchanges: ½ starch, 1½ vegetable, 2 fat

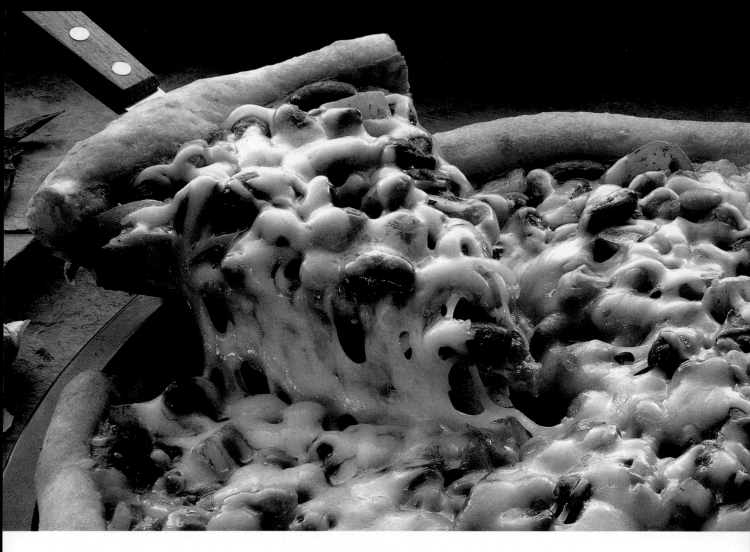

Seasoned Kidney & Pinto Beans

1 medium green pepper, chopped (1 cup)
½ cup chopped red onion
1 teaspoon olive oil
1 can (16 oz.) pinto beans, rinsed and drained
1 can (15½ oz.) dark red kidney beans, rinsed and drained
1 tablespoon lemon juice
½ teaspoon paprika
½ teaspoon dried dill weed or cumin seed
½ teaspoon salt
¼ teaspoon garlic powder

How to Microwave Seasoned Kidney & Pinto Beans

Combine green pepper, onion and oil in 2-quart casserole. Cover. Microwave at High for 4 to 6 minutes, or until vegetables are tender, stirring once. Add remaining ingredients. Mix well. Re-cover. Microwave at High for 3 to 5 minutes, or until mixture is very hot, stirring once or twice. Mash beans slightly with fork.

Spicy Bean Pizza ▲

1 recipe Seasoned Kidney & Pinto Beans (left)
1 pkg. (10 oz.) refrigerated pizza crust dough
1 can (8 oz.) pizza sauce
2 cups shredded mozzarella cheese

6 servings

Prepare beans as directed. Set aside. Heat conventional oven to 425°F. Grease 12-inch pizza pan. Press dough into prepared pan. Bake for 5 to 7 minutes, or just until crust begins to brown. Spread sauce evenly over crust. Spread bean mixture evenly over sauce. Sprinkle with cheese. Bake conventionally for 10 to 13 minutes, or until crust is brown and cheese is melted.

Per Serving: Calories: 400 • Protein: 23 g.
• Carbohydrate: 53 g. • Fat: 11 g.
• Cholesterol: 20 mg. • Sodium: 800 mg.
Exchanges: 3 starch, 1½ medium-fat meat, 1½ vegetable, ½ fat

Bean & Cheese Quesadillas ▲

 1 recipe Seasoned Kidney & Pinto Beans
    (opposite)
 6 flour tortillas (8-inch)
¾ cup shredded Co-Jack cheese
    Vegetable oil
    Shredded lettuce

6 servings

Prepare beans as directed. Spread ½ cup bean
mixture over half of 1 tortilla, to within ½ inch of
edge. Sprinkle with 2 tablespoons cheese. Fold
tortilla over bean mixture. Press lightly to enclose.
Repeat with remaining bean mixture, tortillas
and cheese. In 12-inch skillet, heat ⅛ inch oil
conventionally over medium-high heat. Fry 2
quesadillas at a time for 3 to 5 minutes, or until
golden brown, turning once. Add additional oil,
if necessary. Cut each quesadilla in wedges;
serve on bed of shredded lettuce. Top with sour
cream and chopped tomato, if desired.

Per Serving: Calories: 380 • Protein: 15 g. • Carbohydrate: 50 g.
• Fat: 14 g. • Cholesterol: 13 mg. • Sodium: 460 mg.
Exchanges: 3 starch, ½ medium-fat meat, 1 vegetable, 2 fat

Pinto Bean & Spinach Bake

 3 slices bacon, cut into ½-inch pieces
½ cup chopped onion
 1 clove garlic, minced
½ teaspoon chili powder
¼ teaspoon crushed red pepper flakes
 8 cups torn fresh spinach leaves
 2 cans (15 oz. each) pinto beans with
    jalapeño peppers, rinsed and drained
1½ cups shredded Monterey Jack cheese

4 servings

In 2-quart casserole, combine bacon, onion,
garlic, chili powder and red pepper flakes.
Microwave at High for 5 to 6 minutes, or until
bacon is brown and crisp, stirring once. Add
spinach. Cover. Microwave at High for 2 to 3
minutes, or until spinach is wilted. Add beans
and cheese. Mix well. Microwave at High, uncovered, for 7 to 10 minutes, or until mixture is
hot and cheese is melted, stirring twice.

Per Serving: Calories: 390 • Protein: 26 g. • Carbohydrate: 40 g.
• Fat: 16 g. • Cholesterol: 42 mg. • Sodium: 400 mg.
Exchanges: 2 starch, 2 medium-fat meat, 2 vegetable, 1 fat

Start with Potatoes

Enrich the good vegetable protein of potatoes with eggs, milk or cheese and turn the popular potato into a hearty main dish. For full-meal twice-baked potatoes, try this microwave shortcut. A few minutes in your microwave oven cuts conventional baking time in half, so you can have the crisp, dry skin of oven-baked potatoes, super-quick.

Super-quick Oven-baked Potatoes

4 baking potatoes (8 to 10 oz. each)

How to Make Super-quick Oven-baked Potatoes

Heat conventional oven to 375°F. Pierce potatoes with fork. Arrange in circle on paper towel in microwave oven. Microwave at High for 8 minutes, turning over once. Place potatoes in conventional oven. Bake conventionally for 20 to 25 minutes, or until tender.

◄ Vegetable-stuffed Bakers

1 recipe Super-quick Oven-baked Potatoes (left)	¼ teaspoon salt
¼ cup milk	⅛ teaspoon pepper
¼ cup sour cream	½ cup shredded Monterey Jack cheese
2 tablespoons margarine or butter	2 cups frozen broccoli cuts
¼ teaspoon garlic powder	½ cup chopped red pepper
	⅓ cup chopped onion

4 servings

Prepare potatoes as directed. Cut thin slice from top of each potato. Scoop out pulp, leaving about ¼-inch shell. Set shells aside.

Place pulp in medium mixing bowl. Add milk, sour cream, margarine, garlic powder, salt and pepper. Beat at medium speed of electric mixer until blended. Stir in cheese. Set aside.

In 2-quart casserole, combine remaining ingredients. Cover. Microwave at High for 3 to 5 minutes, or until vegetables are tender-crisp, stirring once. Add to potato mixture. Stir gently to combine. Spoon mixture evenly into potato shells. Arrange potatoes on baking sheet. Place under conventional broiler, 2 to 3 inches from heat. Broil for 4 to 5 minutes, or until browned.

Per Serving: Calories: 350 • Protein: 11 g. • Carbohydrate: 47 g. • Fat: 14 g.
• Cholesterol: 20 mg. • Sodium: 320 mg.
Exchanges: 2½ starch, ½ medium-fat meat, 2 vegetable, 2 fat

Egg-stuffed Potatoes Florentine*

- 1 recipe Super-quick Oven-baked Potatoes (page 147)
- 1/3 cup milk
- 2 tablespoons margarine or butter
- 1 pkg. (9 oz.) frozen chopped spinach
- 1/2 cup shredded Swiss cheese
- 1/4 cup grated Parmesan cheese
- 1/4 teaspoon ground nutmeg (optional)
- 1/4 teaspoon salt
- 4 medium eggs

4 servings

*Recipe not recommended for ovens with less than 600 cooking watts.

Per Serving: Calories: 410 • Protein: 20 g.
• Carbohydrate: 46 g. • Fat: 17 g.
• Cholesterol: 233 mg. • Sodium: 490 mg.
Exchanges: 2½ starch, 1 medium-fat meat,
2 vegetable, 2½ fat

How to Make Egg-stuffed Potatoes Florentine

Prepare potatoes as directed. Cut thin slice from top of each potato. Scoop out pulp, leaving about 1/4-inch shell. Set shells aside.

Place pulp in medium mixing bowl. Add milk and margarine. Beat at medium speed of electric mixer until blended. Set mixture aside.

Microwave spinach, covered, in 1-quart casserole at High for 4 to 6 minutes, or until defrosted. Drain, pressing to remove excess moisture.

Add spinach and remaining ingredients, except eggs, to potato mixture. Mix well. Spoon mixture evenly into potato shells.

Make deep indentation in center of each potato, using back of spoon. Arrange potatoes in 9-inch round cake dish. Place 1 egg in each indentation.

Prick yolks once with wooden pick. Cover with plastic wrap. Microwave at 70% (Medium High) for 12 to 18 minutes, or until egg whites are firm and yolks are almost set, rotating every 3 minutes.

149

Ranch-style Baked Potatoes*

1 recipe Super-quick Oven-
   baked Potatoes (page 147)
¼ cup milk
2 tablespoons margarine or
   butter
½ cup shredded Cheddar
   cheese
2 tablespoons canned
   chopped green chilies
¼ teaspoon garlic powder
¼ teaspoon salt
4 medium eggs
½ cup salsa

4 servings

Prepare potatoes as directed. Cut thin slice from top of each potato. Scoop out pulp, leaving about ¼-inch shell. Set shells aside.
Place pulp in medium mixing bowl. Add milk and margarine. Beat
at medium speed of electric mixer until blended. Add remaining ingredients, except eggs and salsa. Mix well. Spoon mixture evenly
into potato shells. Using back of spoon, make deep indentation in
center of each potato. Arrange potatoes in 9-inch round cake dish.
Place 1 egg in each indentation. Prick yolks once with wooden pick.
Cover with plastic wrap. Microwave at 70% (Medium High) for 12 to
18 minutes, or until egg whites are firm and yolks are almost set, rotating every 3 minutes. Spoon salsa evenly over eggs.

*Recipe not recommended for ovens with less than 600 cooking watts.

Per Serving: Calories: 380 • Protein: 15 g. • Carbohydrate: 45 g. • Fat: 16 g.
• Cholesterol: 229 mg. • Sodium: 600 mg.
Exchanges: 2½ starch, ½ medium-fat meat, 2 vegetable, 2½ fat

Hot Pepper Potato Bake

- 1 pkg. (9 oz.) frozen baby carrots
- 1 lb. new potatoes, thinly sliced
- 1 small onion, thinly sliced
- 2 tablespoons water
- 1 cup cubed fully cooked ham (½-inch cubes)
- ¼ cup margarine or butter, divided
- ¼ cup all-purpose flour
- ¼ teaspoon salt
- 1¼ cups milk
- 2 cups shredded hot pepper cheese
- ½ cup unseasoned dry bread crumbs

4 servings

Heat conventional oven to 400°F. Place carrots in 1-quart casserole. Cover. Microwave at High for 4 to 5 minutes, or until defrosted, stirring once. Drain. Set aside.

In 2-quart casserole, combine potatoes, onion and water. Cover. Microwave at High for 10 to 12 minutes, or until potatoes are tender, stirring once or twice. Drain. Add carrots and ham. Mix well. Set aside.

In 4-cup measure, microwave 2 tablespoons margarine at High for 45 seconds to 1 minute, or until melted. Stir in flour and salt. Blend in milk. Microwave at High for 5 to 6 minutes, or until sauce thickens and bubbles, stirring 3 times. Add cheese. Stir until melted. Pour over potato mixture. Stir to combine. In 2-cup measure, microwave remaining 2 tablespoons margarine at High for 45 seconds to 1 minute, or until melted. Stir in bread crumbs. Sprinkle evenly over potato mixture. Bake, uncovered, for 15 to 22 minutes, or until mixture is set and topping is golden brown.

Per Serving: Calories: 600 • Protein: 29 g.
• Carbohydrate: 47 g. • Fat: 33 g.
• Cholesterol: 75 mg. • Sodium: 1170 mg.
Exchanges: 2½ starch, 3 medium-fat meat, 1½ vegetable, 3 fat

Take your pick of potato chowders. Green chilies add a hint of heat to both.

White-hot Chili & Potato Chowder ▲

1 lb. red potatoes, peeled and cubed
   (½-inch cubes)
⅓ cup chopped onion
1 can (10¾ oz.) condensed cream of potato
   soup
1 pkg. (10 oz.) frozen cream-style corn
1 can (4 oz.) chopped green chilies
1½ cups milk
¼ teaspoon freshly ground pepper

4 servings

In 2-quart casserole, combine potatoes and
onion. Cover. Microwave at High for 8 to 12 minutes, or until potatoes are tender, stirring twice.
Add remaining ingredients. Cover. Microwave at
High for 8 to 10 minutes, or until hot, stirring 2 or
3 times.

Per Serving: Calories: 260 • Protein: 9 g. • Carbohydrate: 49 g.
• Fat: 4 g. • Cholesterol: 11 mg. • Sodium: 1170 mg.
Exchanges: 2½ starch, 1 vegetable, ½ low-fat milk

Red-hot Chili & Potato Chowder ▲

1 lb. red potatoes, peeled and cubed
   (½-inch cubes)
⅓ cup chopped onion
1 can (14½ oz.) whole tomatoes, cut up and
   undrained
1 can (11¼ oz.) condensed chili beef with
   beans soup
1 pkg. (10 oz.) frozen corn in butter sauce
1 can (4 oz.) chopped green chilies
¼ teaspoon freshly ground pepper

4 servings

In 2-quart casserole, combine potatoes and
onion. Cover. Microwave at High for 8 to 12 minutes, or until potatoes are tender, stirring twice.
Add remaining ingredients. Cover. Microwave at
High for 10 to 12 minutes, or until hot, stirring 2
or 3 times.

Per Serving: Calories: 290 • Protein: 9 g. • Carbohydrate: 52 g.
• Fat: 6 g. • Cholesterol: 8 mg. • Sodium: 1310 mg.
Exchanges: 2½ starch, ½ medium-fat meat, 1 fat

Sweet Potato Pancakes with Harvest Fruit Syrup

Syrup:
- 1 pkg. (8 oz.) mixed dried fruit, cut up
- 1/4 cup water
- 2 tablespoons cornstarch
- 1 1/2 cups orange juice
- 1/4 cup honey
- 1 teaspoon grated orange peel

Pancakes:
- 1 cup mashed cooked sweet potatoes
- 1 cup milk
- 2 eggs, beaten
- 2 tablespoons vegetable oil
- 1 cup all-purpose flour
- 3 teaspoons baking powder
- 1 teaspoon pumpkin pie spice
- 1/4 teaspoon salt

Nonstick vegetable cooking spray

4 servings

In 8-cup measure, combine dried fruit and water. Cover with plastic wrap. Microwave at High for 2 to 3 minutes, or until fruit is plumped and softened, stirring once. Let stand, covered, for 3 minutes. Place cornstarch in 2-cup measure. Blend in juice, honey and peel. Add to fruit. Mix well. Microwave at High for 4 to 5 minutes, or until mixture is thickened and translucent, stirring twice. Set aside.

In medium mixing bowl, combine sweet potatoes, milk, eggs and oil. Mix well with whisk. Add flour, baking powder, pumpkin pie spice and salt. Mix well with whisk. Spray 10-inch skillet with cooking spray. Heat skillet conventionally over medium heat. Pour about 1/3 cup batter into hot skillet. Cook until bubbles form and edges start to dry. Turn over and cook for about 2 to 3 minutes longer, or until set in center. Serve pancakes with syrup.

Per Serving: Calories: 560 • Protein: 12 g. • Carbohydrate: 109 g.
• Fat: 11 g. • Cholesterol: 111 mg. • Sodium: 470 mg.
Exchanges: 3 1/2 starch, 3 1/2 fruit, 2 fat